*Written for the NEW **AQA** Specification*

# Target Science

## Physics
### Foundation Tier

**AQA
Modular
Science**

**OXFORD**
UNIVERSITY PRESS

*Stephen Pople*

# OXFORD
## UNIVERSITY PRESS

Great Clarendon Street, Oxford OX2 6DP

Oxford University Press is a department of the University of Oxford.
It furthers the University's objective of excellence in research, scholarship,
and education by publishing worldwide in

Oxford  New York

Athens  Auckland  Bangkok  Bogotá  Buenos Aires  Cape Town
Chennai  Dar es Salaam  Delhi  Florence  Hong Kong  Istanbul  Karachi
Kolkata  Kuala Lumpur  Madrid  Melbourne  Mexico City  Mumbai  Nairobi
Paris  São Paulo  Shanghai  Singapore  Taipei  Tokyo  Toronto  Warsaw
with associated companies in Berlin  Ibadan

Oxford is a registered trade mark of Oxford University Press
in the UK and in certain other countries

British Library Cataloguing in Publication Data

Data available

ISBN 0-19-914829-5

Typeset in Stone Serif
by Ian Foulis & Associates, Plymouth UK
Printed by
Butler & Tanner Ltd, Frome UK

**Acknowledgements**

(Leslie Garland Picture Library = LGPL, Robert Harding Picture Library = RGPL, Science Photo Library = SPL; l = left, r = right, t = top, c = centre, b = bottom.)
Cover SPL; 11l Philip Mould, Historical Portraits Ltd, London UK/Bridgeman Art Library; 11r Frank Zullo/SPL; 12l Russell Cheyne/Allsport; 16/17 Charles & Josette Lenars/Corbis; 18 Superstock; 19l Alvey & Towers Picture Library; 19r © Tony Arruza/Corbis; 21tr © Paul A. Souders/Corbis; 21bl GDA Applied Energy (Creda); 21br Getty Images Stone; 23 © Frans Lanting/ Minden Pictures/RGPL; 24 Getty Images Stone; 30 © Robert Estall/Corbis; 32 © Michael Kevin Daly/The Stockmarket; 34 Steve Strike/ Outback Photographics; 35tl SPL; 35tr LGPL; 35bl Andrew Lambert/LGPL; 36 Patrick Ward/Corbis; 37 Rosenfeld Images Ltd/SPL; 38l Adam Hart-Davis/SPL; 38b Getty Images Stone; 40 © Bryan F. Teyerson/The Stockmarket; 41 Lowell Georgia/SPL; 44 © Jim Sugar Photography/Corbis; 45 SPL; 47 Edifice; 48tl Layne Kennedy/Corbis; 48tr © Raissa Page/Format; 48b The Purcell Team/Corbis; 49t Allsport/ UK Allsport; 48c John Marshall Mantel/Corbis; 48b Corel Professional Photos; 50tl Holt Studios International; 50tr SPL; 50l Martin Bond/SPL; 50b LondonWaste Ltd; 51l Corbis; 51r Corbis; 58/59 SPL; 60 Getty Images Stone; 61t Collections/Brian Shuel; 63 Andrew Lambert/ LGPL; 64 Charles Winters/SPL; 65 Image Bank; 66 SPL; 70 Kevin R. Morris/Corbis; 72 Wattie Cheung/Camera Press; 75cl © Yoav Levy/Phototake/RGPL; 78 Jeremy Walker/SPL; 79t Alvey & Towers Picture Library; 79b Alvey & Towers Picture Library; 81 Andrew Lambert/LGPL; 84 Will & Deni McIntyre/SPL; 85 www.shoutpictures.com; 86 Mark Wagner/ Flight Collection; 87 Epson; 88tl Jack Hollingsworth/ Corbis; 88tr © Roy Morsch/The Stockmarket; 92 LGPL; 95 Getty Images Stone; 97t Alvey & Towers Picture Library; 97b Andrew Lambert/LGPL; 98 US Dept of Energy/SPL; 99 WildCountry/Corbis; 100t © Tom Ives/The Stockmarket; 100c RGPL; 101c www.shoutpictures.com; 101cl www.shoutpictures.com; 101cr www.shoutpictures.com; 101br SPL; 102t Image Bank; 102b Aircare;; 103 Peter Menzel/SPL; 104t RGPL; 104l Martin Bond/SPL; 105 Hulton Getty; 114/115 Paul A. Souders/Corbis; 116 Michael Steele/Allsport; 117 NASA; 118t © David Lawrence/The Stockmarket; 118l Flight Collection; 125tl Takeshi Takahara/SPL; 125tr Alvey & Towers Picture Library; 125b Chris Cole/Allsport; 126 www.shoutpictures.com; 127 Getty Images Stone; 128 Getty Images Stone; 131t Auto Express; 131b Auto Express; 134 Allsport; 135l © John Walmesley; 135r RGPL; 136t Gray Mortimore/Allsport ; 136b © Tim McKenna/ Stockmarket; 137l Photodisc; 137r Alvey & Towers Picture Library; 139 SPL; 142t NASA/ SPL; 142bl L.Pesek/SPL; 142br SPL; 145tl SPL; 145tr European Space Agency/SPL; 145bl NASA; 145br Ken M. Johns/SPL; 147 Tony Hallas/SPL; 148 © Anglo-Australian Telescope/Royal Observatory Edinburgh; 149 European Southern Observatory; 150t John Welzenbach/TheStockmarket; 150c Tony Duffy/Allsport; 151t Allsport; 151b Clive Brunskill/Allsport; 152tl FPG; 152bl Chris van Lennep, Gallo Images/Corbis; 152br Richard Hamilton Smith/Corbis; 154t Photodisc; 154c NASA; 154b NASA; 155 ©Jonathan Blair/Corbis; 164/165 Michael & Patricia Fogden/Corbis; 166 Pete Turner/Image Bank; 169bl Andrew Lambert / LGPL; 169br Andrew Lambert / LGPL; 170 Getty Images Stone; 171t © Chris Rogers/The Stockmarket; 171b Auto Express; 172 Philip James Corwin/Corbis; 174 Andrew Lambert/LGPL; 175 Raymond Gehman/Corbis; 177l Superstock; 177r Dr K. Schiller/SPL; 178c Adam-Hart Davis/SPL; 178b © William Taufic/The Stockmarket; 179 Corel Professional Pictures; 181 Alfred Pasieka/SPL; 184 Keith Kent/SPL ; 186l David Lees/Corbis; 186r Neal Preston/Corbis; 187 Moshe Shai/Corbis; 191 S. Morgan/Frank Spooner; 192t Klaus Guldbrandsen/SPL; 192b Rex Features; 196 © Yoav Levy/Phototake/RGPL; 197 © Werner Forman/Corbis; 199 CERN; 200 N. N. Birks/Ardea; 201 © Yoav Levy/Phototake/RGPL; 202 Roger Ressmeyer /Corbis; 204t Paul A. Souders/Corbis; 204c David H. Wells/Corbis; 204b Jan Butchofsky-Houser/Corbis; 205 Henry Diltz//Corbis; 206 Luis F. Rodriguez; 207tr G. & M. David de Lossy/Image Bank; 208 SPL; 209l Mere Words/SPL; 209r UKAEA

Any uncredited images are from the OUP archive, Peter Gould, or Andrew Lambert.

The publisher wishes to acknowledge the help of Brian Arnold in the preparation of the questions.

# Introduction

Science is about asking questions. Physics is the science that asks questions about the physical world around you, its practical uses, and some of the social issues it raises.

You will find this book useful if you are studying physics as part of the AQA Modular Science Single or Double Award GCSE science course.

Everything in this book has been organized to help you find out things quickly and easily. It is written in two-page units called spreads.

## Use the contents page

If you are looking for information on a large topic, look it up in the contents page.

## Use the index

If there is something small you want to check on, look up the most likely word in the index. The index gives the page number where you'll find information about that word.

## Use the questions

Asking questions and answering them is a very good way of learning. There are questions at the end of every Module. At the end of the book there is a set of further exam-style questions and a selection of multiple-choice questions. Answers to numerical questions, and some pointers to those requiring short answers, are provided.

## Use the key words glossary

At the end of each Module there are a selection of key words and their meanings to help you understand the main ideas given in the Module.

## Helping you revise

To help you revise, in addition to the questions, and the end-of-Module glossaries of important terms, there are some revision notes and some further exam-style questions.

Physics is an important and exciting subject. It doesn't just happen in laboratories. It is all around you: in fairgrounds, fields, farms, and factories. It is taking place deep in the Earth and far out in space. You'll find physics everywhere.

I hope that this book helps you with your studies, that you enjoy using it, and that at the end of your course, you agree with me!

*Stephen P*
*July*

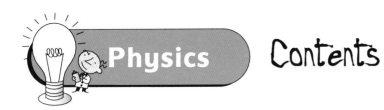

# Physics

# Contents

*Note:* The Further Topics are included to satisfy the additional statutory requirements of the national curriculums for students in Northern Ireland and Wales.

# Routemaps

Although you will probably work through the AQA Specification Module by Module, these *Routemaps* offer alternative pathways through topics and have been constructed to help you 'understand' concepts in small, logical sections. They are particularly useful when revising as they help you identify and revise small sections at a time. They are also helpful to use to catch up if for any reason you have missed any work.

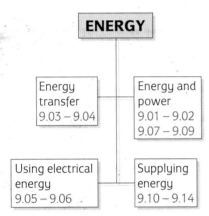

**ENERGY**

Energy transfer
9.03 – 9.04

Energy and power
9.01 – 9.02
9.07 – 9.09

Using electrical energy
9.05 – 9.06

Supplying energy
9.10 – 9.14

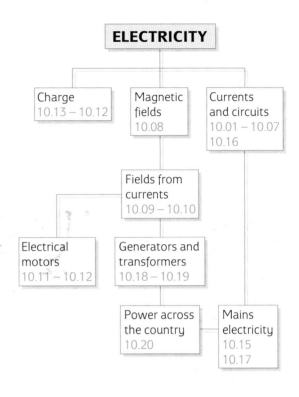

**ELECTRICITY**

Charge
10.13 – 10.12

Magnetic fields
10.08

Currents and circuits
10.01 – 10.07
10.16

Fields from currents
10.09 – 10.10

Electrical motors
10.11 – 10.12

Generators and transformers
10.18 – 10.19

Power across the country
10.20

Mains electricity
10.15
10.17

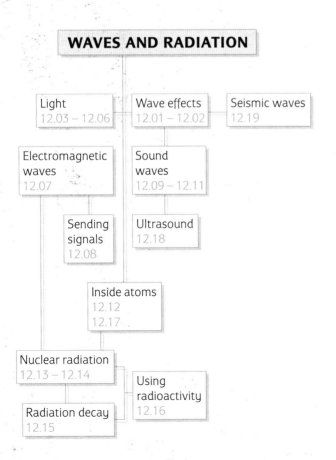

**WAVES AND RADIATION**

Light
12.03 – 12.06

Wave effects
12.01 – 12.02

Seismic waves
12.19

Electromagnetic waves
12.07

Sound waves
12.09 – 12.11

Sending signals
12.08

Ultrasound
12.18

Inside atoms
12.12
12.17

Nuclear radiation
12.13 – 12.14

Using radioactivity
12.16

Radiation decay
12.15

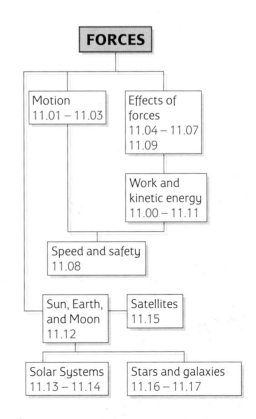

**FORCES**

Motion
11.01 – 11.03

Effects of forces
11.04 – 11.07
11.09

Work and kinetic energy
11.00 – 11.11

Speed and safety
11.08

Sun, Earth, and Moon
11.12

Satellites
11.15

Solar Systems
11.13 – 11.14

Stars and galaxies
11.16 – 11.17

# Getting started

# A system of units

## Objectives

**This spread should help you to**
- give the SI units of mass, length, and time
- say what kilo, milli, and micro mean

mass

length

time

*You can measure the mass of a small object using a **balance** like this one.*

People measure things using many different units, including those shown above. But in scientific work, life is much easier if everyone uses a common system of units.

Most scientists use **SI units** (full name: Système International d'Unités). This system starts with the kilogram, metre, and second – for measuring mass, length, and time. From these come a whole range of units for measuring volume, speed, force, energy, and other quantities.

On the opposite page, there is more information about the kilogram, metre, and second, and bigger and smaller units based on them.

## Bigger and smaller

You can make a unit bigger or smaller by putting an extra symbol, called a **prefix**, in front (in the chart below, W stands for **watt**, the SI unit of power):

## Questions

1 What is the SI unit of mass?
2 What is the SI unit of length?
3 What is the SI unit of time?
4 What do the following stand for?
   kilo    milli    micro
5 Which is the greater:
   **a** 1600 g or 1.5 kg?
   **b** 1250 mm or 1.3 m?

| Prefix | Meaning | Example |
|--------|---------|---------|
| M (mega) | × 1000 000 | MW (megawatt) |
| k (kilo) | × 1000 | km (kilometre) |
| d (deci) | $\times \frac{1}{10}$ | dm (decimetre) |
| c (centi) | $\times \frac{1}{100}$ | cm (centimetre) |
| m (milli) | $\times \frac{1}{1000}$ | mm (millimetre) |
| μ (micro) | $\times \frac{1}{1000 000}$ | μW (microwatt) |

*Note: milli means 'thousandth', not millionth; micro means 'millionth'.*

**Mass** Mass is the amount of matter in something.
The SI unit of mass is the **kilogram** (symbol kg).
You can measure the mass of a small object using a **balance**
like the one in the photograph on the opposite page.

milligram (mg)

hair

1000 mg = 1 g

gram (g)

bank note

1000 g = 1 kg

kilogram (kg)

Sugar

tonne (t)

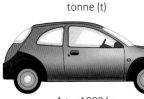

1 t = 1000 kg

**Length** The SI unit of length is the **metre** (symbol m).

micrometre (µm)

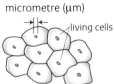

living cells

1000 000 µm = 1 m

millimetre (mm)

1000 mm = 1 m

centimetre (cm)

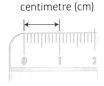

100 cm = 1 m

metre (m)

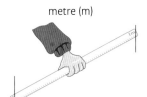

kilometre (km)

1 km = 1000 m

**Time** The SI unit of time is the **second** (symbol s).
For shorter times, the **millisecond** (symbol ms) is
sometimes used: 1000 ms = 1s

## Questions

**6** Copy and complete this table:

|  | Unit | Symbol |
|---|---|---|
| Length | ? | m |
| ? | kilogram | ? |
| Time | ? | ? |

**7** What do the following stand for?

g    mm    mg    t    ms    µm

**8** 10    100    1000    100 000    1000 000
Which of the above is:
**a** the number of mg in 1 g?
**b** the number of mm in 1 cm?
**c** the number of cm in 1 m?
**d** the number of cm in 1 km?
**e** the number of mm in 1 km?

**9** Write down the value of:
**a** 1 m in mm.     **b** 1.5 m in mm.
**c** 1.534 m in mm.     **d** 1652 mm in m.

**10** Write down the value of:
**a** 1 kg in g.     **b** 1750 g in kg.
**c** 26 t in kg.     **d** 6 s in ms.

# S3

# Measuring matters

Over the centuries, people have used a wide variety of units for making measurements. Here are some examples.

## STRANGE but true!

The **foot** (unit of length) was originally the length of a Roman's foot. But some people had much longer feet than others! So, in the 12th century the foot was defined by a law issued by Henry I of England as the total width of 36 ears of barleycorn.

The **acre** (unit of area) was the area of a field that could be ploughed in one day by a team of two oxen.

The **knot** (unit of speed) is still used by mariners at sea and by pilots. It is 1.15 m.p.h., or about 0.5 metres per second. Speed at sea was originally measured by letting a knotted rope out behind the boat and seeing how many knots floated away from the ship in a set time.

The **hand** (unit of length) is the width of an average hand. It is still used for measuring the height of horses.

12 inches = 1 foot
3 feet = 1 yard
22 yards = 1 chain
10 chains = 1 furlong
8 furlongs = 1 mile

# The METRIC system

Most scientists now use units based on the metric system. This was introduced by French scientists in the 1790s, after the French Revolution. It sorted out the muddled systems of units used before by basing everything on the number 10.

The **metre** (unit of length) was defined as one forty millionth of the Earth's circumference. The standard metre was a bar with two marks on it, kept in Paris.

The **gram** (unit of mass) was defined as the mass of one cubic centimetre of water.

# Setting new standards

The original definitions of the metric system are not accurate enough for modern scientific work. For example, a 'standard' metre bar will expand and contract slightly if its temperature varies, so it isn't really standard at all! That is why scientists have had to come up with new and better ways of defining units. Here, for example, is the modern definition of the metre:

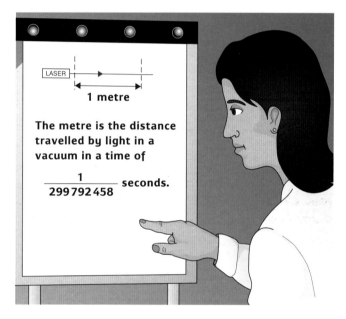

Of course, to define the metre like this, you have to have an exact definition of the second, and that is complicated. It is based on the rate of a vibration which can occur in a certain type of caesium atom.

## Talking points

Scientists use SI units, based on the metric system. For example, the metre is a unit. The *quantity* it measures is length.

Look up the following units in the index in this book. Find out what quantity each one measures:

newton    joule    ohm    ampere    watt

1   Copy and complete the table shown below.

| Measurement | Unit | Symbol |
|---|---|---|
| Length | ? | ? |
| Mass | ? | ? |
| ? | ? | s |
| ? | Ampere | ? |
| Temperature | ? | ? |
| Area | — | ? |
| ? | — | m³ |
| ? | Newton | ? |

2   **a**  How many mg are there in 1 g?
   **b**  How many g are there in 1 kg?
   **c**  How many mg are there in 1 kg?
   **d**  How many mm are there in 4 km?
   **e**  How many cm are there in 5 km?

3   Write down the values of:
   **a**  300 cm in    m
   **b**  500 g in     kg
   **c**  1500 m in    km
   **d**  250 ms in    s
   **e**  0.5 s in     ms
   **f**  0.75 km in   m
   **g**  2.5 kg in    g
   **h**  0.8 m in     mm

4   Copy and complete the table shown below.

| Length | Width | Height | Volume of rectangular block |
|---|---|---|---|
| 2 cm | 3 cm | 4 cm | ? |
| 5 cm | 5 cm | ? | 100 cm³ |
| 6 cm | ? | 5 cm | 300 cm³ |
| ? | 10 cm | 10 cm | 500 cm³ |

5   Calculate the density of the following:
   **a**  a piece of steel which has a volume of 6 cm³ and a mass of 48g.
   **b**  a piece of copper which has a volume of 10 cm³ and a mass of 90 g.
   **c**  a piece of gold which has a volume of 2.0 cm³ and a mass of 38 g.

6   Calculate the mass of the following:
   **a**  4 cm³ of aluminium. The density of aluminium is 2.7 g/cm³.
   **b**  20 cm³ of wood. The density of wood is 0.80 g/cm³.
   **c**  80 cm³ of glass. The density of glass is 2.5 g/cm³.

7   Calculate the volume of the following:
   **a**  68 g of mercury. The density of mercury is 13.6 g/cm³.
   **b**  15.8 g of iron. The density of iron is 7.9 g/cm³.
   **c**  99 g of lead. The density of lead is 11 g/cm³.

# Key words

*The spread numbers in brackets tell you where to find more information.*

**density**    If a material with a mass of 1000 kg has a volume of 1 cubic metre, then its density is 1000 $kg/m^3$. *(0.02, 12.19)*

**kilogram (kg)**    Unit of mass. *(0.01)*

**mass**    The amount of matter in something. It is measured in kilograms (kg). *(0.01)*

**metre (m)**    Unit of length. 1000 metres equals 1 kilometre (km). *(0.01)*

**second (s)**    Unit of time. *(0.01)*

**volume**    The amount of space something takes up. It is measured in cubic metres ($m^3$). A smaller unit of volume is the cubic centimetre ($cm^3$), or millilitre (ml).

$$1\,cm^3 = 1\,ml = \frac{1}{1\,000\,000\,m^3}.$$

*(0.02)*

# Energy

# Module 9

The Niagara falls, on the USA–Canada border. The photograph shows the highest section of the falls, where the water tumbles over 30 metres to the river below. Nearly three million litres of water flow over the falls every second. Most of the energy is wasted, but some is harnessed by a hydroelectric power station which generates electricity for the surrounding area.

# Energy

*This tennis player is using up energy.*

You use **energy** when you climb the stairs, lift a bag, or hit a tennis ball. Energy is used whenever a force makes something move. The greater the force, and the further it moves, the more energy is used.

Energy must also be used to heat things. Everything is made of tiny particles, such as atoms. These are constantly on the move. To increase the temperature of something, it must be given more energy to make its particles move faster.

## Measuring energy

Energy is measured in **joules** (J). For many energy measurements, the joule is rather a small unit. Larger units of energy, based on the joule, are the **kilojoule** and the **megajoule**:

1 kilojoule (kJ)  =  1000 J      1 megajoule (MJ)  =  1000 000 J

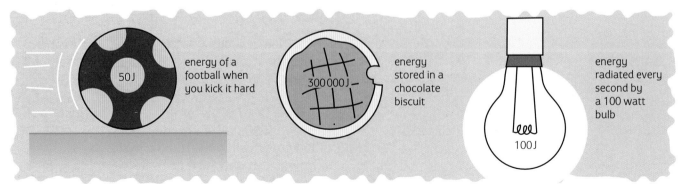

50 J — energy of a football when you kick it hard

300 000 J — energy stored in a chocolate biscuit

100 J — energy radiated every second by a 100 watt bulb

## Forms of energy

Energy can exist in different forms. These are described in the chart at the top of the next page.

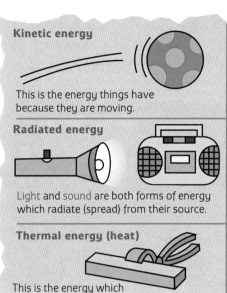

**Kinetic energy**

This is the energy things have because they are moving.

**Radiated energy**

Light and sound are both forms of energy which radiate (spread) from their source.

**Thermal energy (heat)**

This is the energy which comes from hot things when they cool down.

**Potential energy**

This is stored energy. Here are some examples:

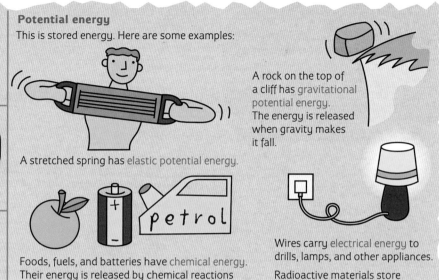

A stretched spring has elastic potential energy.

Foods, fuels, and batteries have chemical energy. Their energy is released by chemical reactions (for example, by burning a fuel).

A rock on the top of a cliff has gravitational potential energy. The energy is released when gravity makes it fall.

Wires carry electrical energy to drills, lamps, and other appliances.

Radioactive materials store nuclear energy.

## Thermal energy (heat) is not the same as temperature:

*The sparks from this sparkler are at a temperature of 1600 °C. But they hold so little energy that they do not burn you when they touch your skin.*

*This molten (melted) iron is also at 1600 °C. It holds lots of energy and would be very dangerous to touch.*

## Questions

1  What unit is used for measuring energy?
2  Give *two* examples of things whose stored energy can be released by chemical reactions.
3  Look at the diagram on the opposite page, showing the football, chocolate biscuit, and bulb.

a  What form of energy does the moving football have?

b  How much energy does the chocolate biscuit store, in kilojoules (kJ)?

c  How much energy does the light bulb radiate in one minute?

# Energy changes

Energy doesn't vanish when you use it. It just goes somewhere else! The diagram below is an example of how energy can change from one form to another. It is sometimes called an **energy chain**:

In every energy chain, the total amount of energy stays the same. Scientists express this idea in the **law of conservation of energy**:

Energy can change into different forms, but it cannot be made or destroyed.

| chemical energy | → | kinetic energy | → | gravitational potential energy | → | kinetic energy | → | thermal energy (heat) |

Above, when the weights hit the ground, they make the atoms and molecules in the ground – and themselves – move a little faster. So their kinetic energy is changed into thermal energy (heat). In any chain, energy is always wasted as heat. For example, you give off heat when you exercise, which is why you sweat! However, the *total* amount of energy (including the heat) stays the same.

## Energy changers

Here are some examples of energy changers in action:

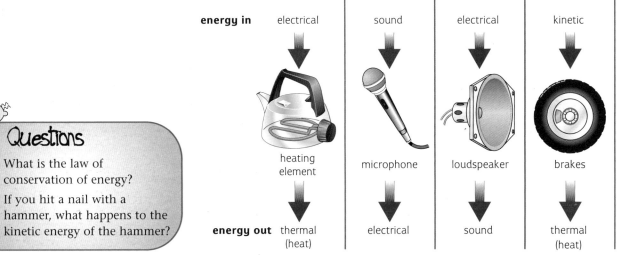

| energy in | electrical | sound | electrical | kinetic |
| | heating element | microphone | loudspeaker | brakes |
| energy out | thermal (heat) | electrical | sound | thermal (heat) |

**Questions**

1 What is the law of conservation of energy?

2 If you hit a nail with a hammer, what happens to the kinetic energy of the hammer?

## Storing and changing energy

Some things are useful because they store energy which can then be changed into other forms. Here are some examples:

*In this clockwork radio, a spring stores energy when you wind it up. As the spring slowly unwinds, it turns a generator which produces an electric current for the radio.*

*Plants take in energy from sunlight. The energy is stored in their roots and leaves as they grow. Animals (like us) can get this energy by eating plants.*

*This night storage heater stores energy when bricks inside it are heated up overnight, by electric elements, using cheap electricity. The heat is slowly released through the day.*

*The gas in the canister stores energy which is released when the gas burns in the air.*

## Questions

**3** *pole vaulter    sprinter    electric toaster    battery*
Which of the above:
**a** changes electrical energy into thermal energy (heat)?
**b** changes kinetic energy into gravitational potential energy?
**c** changes chemical energy into kinetic energy?

**4** Scientists say that energy can 'never be destroyed'. Explain what they mean.

**5** When a rock falls off a cliff and hits the ground, the energy changes could be shown like this:

gravitational potential energy $\rightarrow$ kinetic energy $\rightarrow$ thermal energy (heat)

Show the energy changes which happen when:
**a** you apply the brakes on a cycle and make it stop.
**b** you wind up a clockwork radio and then listen to it.

# Conduction and convection

## Thermal conduction

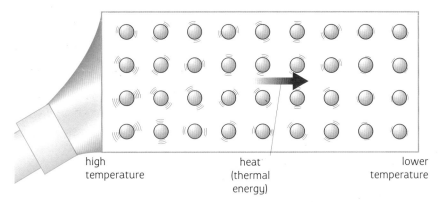

high temperature     heat (thermal energy)     lower temperature

All materials are made up of tiny, moving particles (atoms or molecules). The higher the temperature, the faster they move. If one end of a metal bar is heated, as above, heat (**thermal energy**) is transferred from the hot end to the cold as the faster particles pass on their extra movement to those all along the bar. The energy is travelling by **thermal conduction** (or **conduction**, for short).

Metals are the best **conductors** of heat. Non-metal solids tend to be poor conductors, and so do most liquids. Gases are the worst of all. Bad conductors are called **insulators**. Many materials are insulators because they contain pockets of trapped air.

| Good conductors | | |
|---|---|---|
| metals | e.g. | copper |
| | | aluminium |
| | | iron |
| silicon | | |
| graphite | | |

| Poor conductors (insulators) | |
|---|---|
| glass | |
| water | |
| plastics | |
| rubber | |
| wood | |
| materials containing trapped air | wool |
| | glass wool (fibreglass) |
| | plastic foam |
| | expanded polystyrene |

*The materials above are arranged in order of conducting ability, starting with the best.*

## Convection

Liquids and gases are poor conductors, but if they are free to circulate, they can carry heat with them. There is an example below. Here, the air in a room is being warmed by a heater. The warm air rises as cooler, denser air sinks and displaces it (pushes it out of the way). The result is a circulating stream, called a **convection** current. This carries heat to other parts of the room.

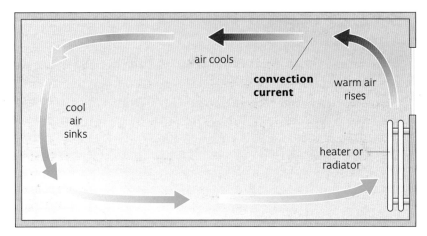

air cools

**convection current**

warm air rises

cool air sinks

heater or radiator

Convection can also happen in liquids. For example, hot water rises when it is displaced by cooler, denser water sinking around it. That is why, in a hot water storage tank like the one in the diagram below, the hottest water collects at the top.

## Using insulating materials

In a house, good insulation means lower fuel bills. Below, you can see some of the ways in which insulating materials are used to reduce heat losses:

*Feathers are a good thermal insulator, especially when fluffed up to trap more air.*

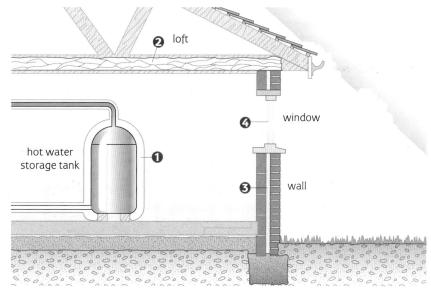

1  Plastic foam lagging round the hot water storage tank.
2  Glass or mineral wool insulation in the loft.
3  Wall cavity filled with plastic foam, beads, or mineral wool.
4  Double-glazed windows: two sheets of glass with air between.

Some insulating materials have a shiny, metallic coating to reduce heat losses by thermal radiation (explained in the next spread).

## Questions

1  Which materials are the best conductors?

2  Why are wool and feathers good insulators?

3  Explain each of the following:

   **a** A saucepan might have a copper bottom but a plastic handle.

   **b** Someone feels cold in a string vest, but warm if they wear a tight shirt over it.

   **c** It is safer picking up hot dishes with a dry cloth than a wet one.

4  Explain each of the following:

   **a** A radiator quickly warms all the air in a room, even though air is a poor thermal conductor.

   **b** Anyone standing near a bonfire feels a draught.

   **c** If a hot water storage tank has an immersion heater (electric heating element), this is fitted near the bottom of the tank rather than near the top.

5  Give *three* ways in which insulating materials are used to reduce heat losses from a house.

# Thermal radiation

## Objectives

**This spread should help you to**

- explain what surfaces are best at emitting and absorbing thermal radiation
- describe how a solar panel and a vacuum flask work

On Earth, we are warmed by the Sun. Its energy travels to us as tiny **electromagnetic waves**. These include invisible **infrared** waves as well as light, and they can travel through empty space. They heat up things that absorb them, so are often called **thermal radiation**.

All things emit (send out) some thermal radiation. The hotter they are, the more energy they radiate per second.

## Emitters and absorbers

Some surfaces are better at emitting thermal radiation than others. The chart on the next page shows how surfaces compare. Good emitters of radiation are also good absorbers. White or silvery surfaces are poor absorbers because they reflect most of the radiation away. That is why, in hot, sunny countries, houses are often painted white to keep them cool inside.

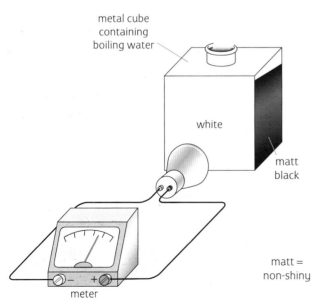

**Comparing emitters** *The metal cube is filled with boiling water. This heats the surfaces to the same temperature. The thermal radiation detector is placed in turn at the same distance from each surface and the meter readings compared.*

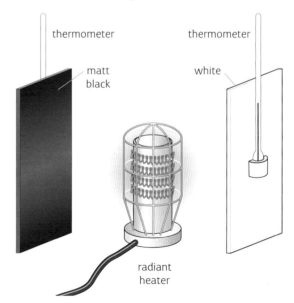

**Comparing absorbers** *The metal plates are placed at the same distance from a radiant heater. To find out which surface absorbs thermal radiation quickest, the rises in temperature are compared.*

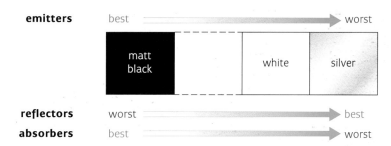

| emitters | best | → | worst |
|----------|------|---|-------|

| matt black | | white | silver |
|------------|---|-------|--------|

| reflectors | worst | → | best |
|------------|-------|---|------|
| absorbers | best | → | worst |

*This chart shows how some surfaces compare as emitters, reflectors, and absorbers of thermal radiation.*

## The solar panel

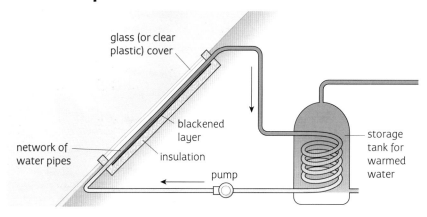

glass (or clear plastic) cover
blackened layer
network of water pipes
insulation
pump
storage tank for warmed water

The **solar panel** above uses the Sun's thermal radiation to warm up water for the house. The blackened layer absorbs the radiant energy and warms the water flowing through the pipes.

## The vacuum flask

A vacuum flask can keep drinks hot (or cold) for hours. It has these features for reducing how quickly energy flows out (or in):

1 A stopper to reduce convection (hot air rising).
2 A double-walled container with a gap between the walls. Air has been removed from the gap to reduce conduction.
3 Walls with silvery surfaces to reduce thermal radiation.

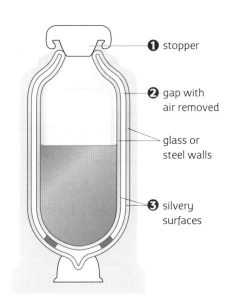

❶ stopper

❷ gap with air removed

glass or steel walls

❸ silvery surfaces

*A vacuum flask.*

## Questions

1 *white    silvery    matt black*
   Which of the above surfaces is the best at:
   **a** absorbing thermal radiation?
   **b** emitting thermal radiation?
   **c** reflecting thermal radiation?
2 Why does the solar panel above have:
   **a** a blackened layer at the back?
   **b** a network of water pipes?

3 What feature does a vacuum flask have to stop it losing (or gaining) heat by thermal radiation?
4 Explain why:
   **a** In hot countries, houses are often painted white.
   **b** On a hot summer's day, if cars are left in a car park, the inside of a white car is cooler than a black one.
   **c** Aluminium foil helps keep food dishes warm when they're out on the table.

# Energy by wire

## Appliances in action

Things like electric irons, vacuum cleaners, toasters, and kettles are called electrical **appliances**. Their job is to take electrical energy from the mains and deliver it in a more useful form. You can see some examples in the chart below. Scientifically speaking, appliances **transform** (or **transfer**) energy – they change it into another form.

Most appliances waste some of the energy supplied to them. The energy is lost as heat (thermal energy). For example, an ordinary light bulb, with a filament, gives off more energy as heat than it does as light.

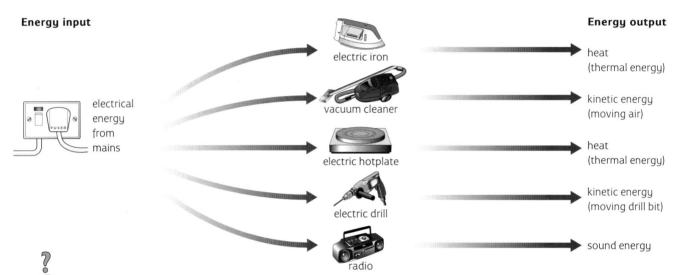

Energy input

electrical energy from mains

electric iron — heat (thermal energy)

vacuum cleaner — kinetic energy (moving air)

electric hotplate — heat (thermal energy)

electric drill — kinetic energy (moving drill bit)

radio — sound energy

Energy output

## Questions

1  electric food mixer
   stereo system
   table lamp
   electric toaster

   Look at the appliances written above. Which appliance is used to change electrical energy into:

   **a** thermal energy (heat)?
   **b** sound energy?
   **c** light energy?
   **d** kinetic energy?

2  Write down *three* more appliances, used in the house or garden, which change electrical energy into kinetic energy.

## Power

Most appliances have a **power** marked on them. This tells you how quickly they take energy from the mains.

Power is measured in **watts** (W). A power of 1 watt means that energy is taken at the rate of 1 joule every second.

So a 100 watt light bulb takes 100 joules of energy every second from the mains.

Sometimes, the power of an appliance is given in **kilowatts** (kW):

  1 kilowatt (kW) = 1000 watts (W)

You can see some examples of power values in the next diagram.

Appliances with heating elements tend to have the highest powers. Electronic equipment such as radio, TVs, and computers usually have least power.

**typical powers**

low power ← → high power

| radio | TV | vacuum cleaner | electric kettle | electric cooker |
|-------|-----|----------------|-----------------|-----------------|
| 10 W | 120 W | 1000 W | 2300 W | 12000 W |

The actual power of an appliance can vary depending on how it is being used. For example, the power figure for the cooker above assumes that the oven, grill, and all the hotplates are all switched on together. Also, if there is a drop in mains voltage for some reason, an appliance will take less power than the stated value. For example, on a lower voltage a bulb will glow more dimly.

If you want to save money on your electricity bill, it is important to know which appliances take most power. The greater the power and the longer the appliance is switched on for, the more energy it takes from the mains, and the more it costs to run.

## Questions

**3** Most of the appliances in question **1** waste some of the energy they take from the mains. For each appliance, write down any other forms of energy that they give out.

**4** The kettle and cooker in the diagram above have powers of 2300 W and 12000 W.

   **a** What does the W stand for?

   **b** How much energy (in joules) does the kettle take from the mains in 1 second?

   **c** How much energy (in joules) does the kettle take from the mains in 10 seconds?

   **d** What is the power of the kettle in kW?

   **e** What is the power of the cooker in kW?

# Buying electricity

**Objectives**

**This spread should help you to**
- calculate energy in kWh
- calculate the cost of running mains appliances

Like other appliances, TVs and hairdriers take energy from the mains. That energy must be paid for, on your electricity bill.

Dan keeps his fan heater on all evening because he feels cold. Chloe uses her stereo player all day. Each thinks that the other is wasting electricity. But who is adding most to the bill? By the end of this spread, you should be able to work it out.

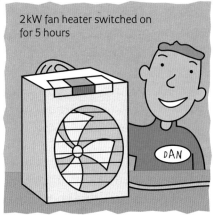

2 kW fan heater switched on for 5 hours

100 W stereo player switched on for 12 hours

## Calculating energy... in joules

A heater with a power of 1 watt (W) uses 1 joule (J) of energy every second. So:

With 1 J of energy, you could run a 1 W heater for 1 second.

With 6 J of energy, you could run a 1 W heater for 6 seconds

...or a 2 W heater for 3 seconds.

In each case, you can calculate the energy in J like this:

| energy | = | power | × | time |
|--------|---|-------|---|------|
| in J | | in W | | in seconds |

## Calculating energy... in kilowatt hours

Electricity supply companies measure energy in **kilowatt hours** (kW h). (1 kW h is 3 600 000 J.) They charge you a set amount for each kW h supplied.

You calculate the energy in kW h like this:

| energy | = | power | × | time |
|--------|---|-------|---|------|
| in kWh | | in kW | | in hours |

For example, if a 3 kW heater is switched on for 4 hours:

energy supplied = 3 × 4 = 12 kW h

The greater the power of the appliance and the longer it is switched on for, the more energy it takes from the mains.

**Questions**

1 *W     J     kWh*

   **a** What do the above stand for?

   **b** Which are units of energy?

2 With 6 joules of energy, how long could you run a 3 watt heater for?

**Did you know?**

**Counting the cost**

If each kWh of energy costs 10p, then it will cost about...

   5p to watch TV all evening

  15p to bake a cake

  30p to wash one load of clothes

240p to run a fan heater all day

*The electricity bill on the right is based on the meter readings below. On many bills there is a standing (fixed) charge as well.*

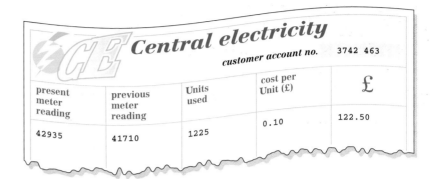

| present meter reading | previous meter reading | Units used | cost per Unit (£) | £ |
|---|---|---|---|---|
| 42935 | 41710 | 1225 | 0.10 | 122.50 |

*customer account no.* 3742 463

meter reading

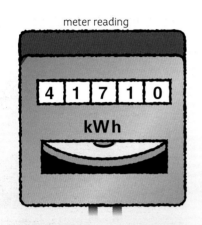

**kWh**

meter reading 3 months later

**kWh**

## Reading the meter

The 'electricity meter' in a house is an energy meter. The more energy you take from the mains, the more you have to pay. The reading on the meter gives the total energy supplied in **Units**. The Unit is another name for the kilowatt hour.

The diagrams on the left show the meter readings at the beginning and end of a quarter (three-month period). In this case, the energy supplied in that period was 1225 Units.

If the electricity supply company charges 10p per Unit (kWh):

cost of energy supplied = $1225 \times 10p = 12\,250p = £122.50$

## Cost problem

**Problem** If the cost of energy is 10p per Unit, how much will it cost to run a 3 kW fan heater for 4 hours?

Using the energy equation on the opposite page:

energy in kWh = 3 kW × 4 hours = 12 kWh = 12 Units

If energy is 10p per Unit: the cost of 12 Units = 12 × 10p = 120p

So, the cost of running the fan heater is 120p (£1.20).

## Questions

**3** Explain why a hairdrier could cost less to run than a table lamp, even though its power is greater.

**4** Use the information in the table on the right to answer the following:

  **a** How much energy does the heater take, in kWh?

  **b** What is the cost of using the heater?

  **c** What is the power of the lamp in kW?

  **d** How much energy does the lamp take, in kWh?

  **e** What is the cost of using the lamp?

| | Power | Time switched on |
|---|---|---|
| heater | 3 kW | 5 hours |
| lamp | 100 W | 12 hours |
| cost per Unit = 10p | | 1 kW = 1000 W |

**5** Look at the information about Dan's fan heater and Chloe's stereo at the start of the spread. Work out which takes most energy from the mains.

## 9.07 Lifting power

### Objectives

**This spread should help you to**

- calculate gravitational potential energy
- do power calculations

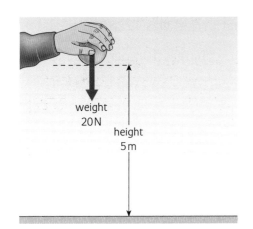

weight
20N

height
5m

### Questions

*Assume that g = 10N/kg*

1 A block of mass 4 kg is lifted 2m above the ground.

  **a** What is the weight of the block in N?

  **b** How much GPE does the block gain?

  **c** If the same block were lifted to twice the original height, how much GPE would it gain?

The crane above is lifting a heavy load above the ground. Like most cranes, this one is powered by an electric motor. So, when it lifts the load, it is changing electrical energy into **gravitational potential energy**, or **GPE** for short.

## Calculating GPE

If something is lifted above the ground, its gain in gravitational potential energy in joules (J) can be calculated like this:

  gain in GPE  = weight × gain in height

The weight is in newtons (N): see the panel on the opposite page for the link between mass in kg and weight in N.

The gain in height is in metres (m), and is measured vertically.

For example, if a stone of weight 20N is lifted 5m above the ground, as on the left:

  gain in GPE  = weight × gain in height = 20 × 5 = 100J

The above equation shows that the GPE is increased if an object has more weight or is lifted higher above the ground.

## GPE and power

A crane's useful power output in watts (W) is the energy in joules (J) it delivers *per second*. If a crane delivers 1000 joules of energy per second, the useful power output is 1000 watts.

There is an example of a power calculation on the right.

30

mass = 1 kg

weight = 10 N

force needed to lift
= 10 N

For more on this, see module 11.

## Mass and weight

Weight is a force, measured in newtons (N). On Earth, each kilogram (kg) of mass weighs 10 newtons: scientifically speaking, the Earth has a **gravitational field strength** of 10 newtons per kilogram (N/kg). This value is called $g$.

So a mass of 1 kg has a weight of 10 N, a mass of 2 kg has a weight of 20 N...and so on.

## Why the GPE equation works

For a force to make something move, work must be done. Work, like energy, is measured in joules (J). It is calculated with this equation:

work done (in J)  =  force (in N) × distance moved (in m)

When a force is used to lift something:

- The work done is equal to the gain in gravitational potential energy (GPE).
- The force must support the weight. So it must *equal* the weight.
- The distance moved is the gain in height.

So, the above equation for 'work done' can be rewritten like this:

gain in GPE (in J)  =  weight (in N) × gain in height (in m)

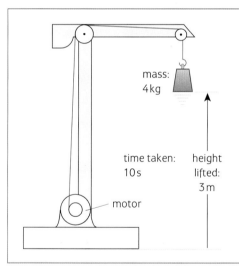

mass:
4 kg

time taken:
10 s

height lifted:
3 m

motor

The model crane on the left can lift a mass of 4 kg through a height of 3 metres in 10 seconds. This is how you would calculate its useful power output:

- Calculate the weight of the object being lifted. (This is 10 N for each kg of mass.)

- Calculate the gain in GPE. This is the crane's useful energy output.

- Divide by the time to find the useful energy output per second. This is the useful power output.

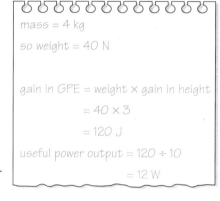

mass = 4 kg

so weight = 40 N

gain in GPE = weight × gain in height
= 40 × 3
= 120 J

useful power output = 120 ÷ 10
= 12 W

## Questions

*Assume that g = 10 N/kg*

**2** An electric motor is used to haul a load weighing 600 N through a vertical height of 10 m in 20 s.

**a** How much gravitational potential energy does the load gain?

**b** How much gravitational potential energy does the load gain every second while it is being lifted?

**c** What is the motor's useful power output?

**d** If the motor had twice the power, what effect do you think this would have?

# Efficiency and power

**This spread should help you to**

- explain what efficiency means, and how it is linked to energy and power

*Human 'engines' (muscles) have an efficiency of about 15%.*

Engines and motors deliver energy by producing motion. To do this, engines get energy by burning their fuel. Electric motors get energy from a battery or generator. Even your body is a type of engine. It gets energy by 'burning up' food, but without flames.

## Efficiency

An engine uses some of the energy put into it to produce motion, but the rest is wasted as heat. In other words, only some of the energy is 'useful'.

The **efficiency** of an engine can be calculated like this:

$$\text{efficiency} = \frac{\text{useful energy output}}{\text{energy input}}$$

For example, if a petrol engine delivers 25 J of useful energy for every 100 J of energy put into it, then its efficiency is 0.25, or 25%.

Here are some typical efficiencies:

| Energy input | | Useful energy output | Efficiency |
|---|---|---|---|
| 100 J | petrol engine | 25 J | 25% |
| 100 J | diesel engine | 35 J | 35% |
| 100 J | electric motor | 80 J | 80%* |

*Although electric motors have a high efficiency, the efficiency of the power stations that generate the electricity for them is only about 35%.

## Engine power

A small engine can deliver as much energy as a big engine, but it takes longer to do it. The big engine delivers energy at a faster rate. In other words, the big engine has more power.

Power is measured in **watts** (W). A power of 1 watt means that energy is being delivered (or *transferred*) at the rate of 1 J per second.

Power can be calculated like this:

$$\text{useful power output} = \frac{\text{useful energy output}}{\text{time taken}}$$

For example, if an engine delivers 1000 joules of useful energy in 2 seconds, its useful power output is 500 watts (500 joules per second).

1 A motor has an *efficiency* of 50%. Explain in words what this means.

2 One engine has twice the *power* of another. Explain in words what this means.

Engine powers are usually given in kilowatts (kW). 1 kW = 1000 W.

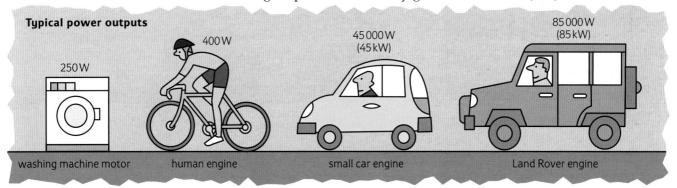

**Typical power outputs**

250 W — washing machine motor

400 W — human engine

45 000 W (45 kW) — small car engine

85 000 W (85 kW) — Land Rover engine

Here is another way of calculating efficiency:

$$\text{efficiency} = \frac{\text{useful power output}}{\text{power input}}$$

For example, the electric motor below has a power input of 600 W, and a useful power output of 480 W. So:

$$\text{efficiency} = \frac{\text{useful power output}}{\text{power input}} = \frac{480}{600} = 0.8 = 80\%$$

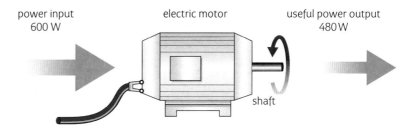

power input 600 W → electric motor → useful power output 480 W

shaft

Of the 600 W supplied to the motor, only 480 W is 'useful' and turns the shaft. The other 120 W is wasted. In other words, 120 joules of energy are lost every second as heat. That is why the motor gets warm when it is working.

## Questions

**3** With each 5000 J of energy supplied to it by its fuel, an engine delivers 2000 J of useful energy.

  **a** What is its efficiency?

  **b** What happens to the rest of the energy supplied?

**4** Human 'engines' (muscles) have an efficiency of about 15%. Explain why this means that you must get hot when you take exercise.

**5** If an engine delivers 800 J of useful energy in 4 s, what is its useful power output in watts?

**6** An electric motor has a useful power output of 3 kW.

  **a** What is its useful power output in watts?

  **b** How much useful energy does it deliver in 1 s?

  **c** If the power input to the motor is 4 kW, what is the efficiency?

# More about efficiency

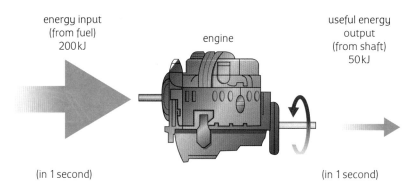

energy input (from fuel) 200 kJ

engine

useful energy output (from shaft) 50 kJ

(in 1 second)

(in 1 second)

$$\text{efficiency} = \frac{\text{useful energy output}}{\text{energy input}} = \frac{50}{200} = 0.25 = 25\%$$

The diagram above is a reminder of what **efficiency** means. This engine has an efficiency of 0.25, or 25%. In other words, only one quarter of the energy from its fuel reaches the shaft as useful energy output. The rest is wasted as heat.

## A problem with energy spreading

Fuel-burning engines aren't very efficient. They waste more energy than they deliver to the wheels of the vehicle. It isn't a matter of poor design. Whenever heat is used to produce motion, some of the energy becomes spread out. This makes it less useful.

Imagine a huge tankful of warm water. It contains lots of energy, but there is no way of concentrating this energy to produce motion. A similar problem happens in the cylinders of an engine. When the hot, burning gases expand, they cool, and their remaining energy becomes too spread out to be of any use. Instead, it is wasted as heat.

*An engine wastes more energy as heat than it delivers to the wheels. In the Australian outback, some drivers use the heat from the engine to cook their food.*

## Lighting efficiency

*A filament bulb has a low efficiency.*

*A low-energy bulb has a high efficiency.*

Ordinary light bulbs contain a tiny tungsten filament (thin wire) which glows white hot when a current flows through it. Bulbs like this are not very efficient. They give off far more energy as heat than they do as light.

Low-energy bulbs use a glowing gas, rather than a filament. They have a very high efficiency. A 20 watt low-energy bulb gives as much light as a 100 watt filament bulb. Fitting low-energy bulbs is a good way of saving money on your electricity bill – and helping the environment by wasting less energy.

Fluorescent tubes work in the same way as low-energy bulbs. They also have a very high efficiency.

*A radio has a low efficiency, but that doesn't really matter.*

## Low efficiency allowed

With some electrical equipment, low efficiency is not a problem. For example, a radio changes only a tiny fraction of its power into sound, but its low efficiency doesn't really matter. Its power consumption is only a few watts. Also, human ears are so sensitive that only a tiny amount of power must come from the loudspeaker for it to sound very loud.

## Questions

1 Look at the diagram at the top of the opposite page. How much energy does the engine waste (in one second)?

2 When fuel burns in an engine, some of the energy released gets spread out. Why is this a problem?

3 Someone claims to have invented an engine with an efficiency of 100%. Explain why you shouldn't believe them.

4 Suggest a reason for each of the following:

  a Light bulbs should have as high an efficiency as possible.

  b Radios have a low efficiency, but this doesn't really matter.

5 Explain why a filament bulb get hotter than a low-energy bulb of the same brightness.

*A coal-burning power station. The large, round towers with clouds of steam coming from them are cooling towers.*

Industrial societies use huge amounts of energy. Much of it is supplied by mains electricity. This comes from **generators** in **power stations**.

## Thermal power stations

Power stations which use heat from a fuel to supply their energy are called **thermal power stations**. The diagram below shows the basic layout of a large thermal power station:

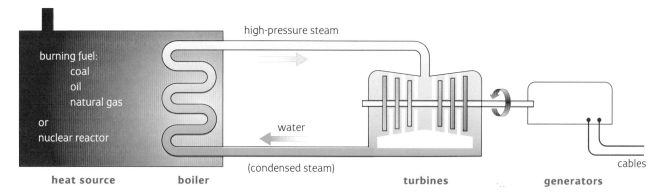

high-pressure steam

burning fuel:
coal
oil
natural gas
or
nuclear reactor

water

(condensed steam)

cables

**heat source**   **boiler**   **turbines**   **generators**

## Questions

1  Write down *four* types of fuel used in thermal power stations.

2  Give one type of thermal power station that does not burn its fuel.

The generators are turned by **turbines**, blown round by high-pressure steam. To produce the steam, water is heated in a boiler. The heat comes from burning fuel (coal, oil, or natural gas) or from a **nuclear reactor**. Nuclear fuel does not burn. Its energy is released by nuclear reactions that split uranium atoms.

Once steam has passed through the turbines, it is cooled, condensed (turned back into a liquid), and fed back to the boiler.

To condense the steam, some power stations have huge cooling towers, with draughts of air up through them, as in the photograph above. Others use the cooling effect of nearby sea or river water.

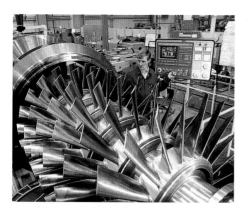

*A turbine from a power station.*

## Efficiency problems

Thermal power stations waste more energy than they deliver. Most is lost as heat in the cooling water and waste gases. For example, the efficiency of a typical coal-burning power station is only about 35% – only about 35% of the energy in its fuel is changed into electrical energy. You can see what happens to the rest in the chart below.

Engineers try to make power stations as efficient as they can. But it is impossible to use all of the heat from the fuel to produce motion. Petrol and diesel engines have the same problem.

The heat from a power station does not all have to be wasted. With long water pipes, some can be used to heat local buildings.

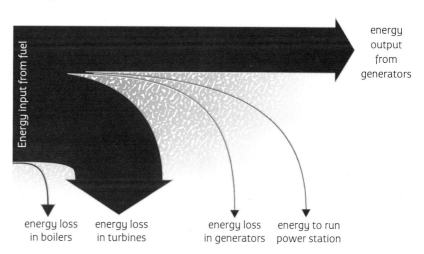

*What happens to the energy in a large thermal power station. The thicker the arrow, the greater the energy. An energy flow chart like this is called a **Sankey diagram**.*

## Questions

3   In a thermal power station:

   **a** Where does the steam come from?

   **b** What is the steam used for?

   **c** What turns the generators?

   **d** What do the cooling towers do?

4   The table on the right gives data about the power input and losses in two power stations, X and Y:

   **a** Where is most energy wasted?

   **b** In what form is this wasted energy lost?

   **c** What is the electrical power output of each station? (Assume that the table shows *all* the power losses in each station.)

**d** Which station has the higher efficiency?

| | Power station | |
| | X | Y |
| | coal | nuclear |
| power input from fuel in MW | 5600 | 5600 |
| power losses in MW: | | |
| – in reactors/boilers | 600 | 200 |
| – in turbines | 2900 | 3800 |
| – in generators | 40 | 40 |
| power to run station in MW | 60 | 60 |
| electrical power output in MW | ? | ? |

# Energy for electricity (2)

## Pollution problems

fuel (coal, oil, or natural gas)

oxygen (from air)

carbon dioxide

water vapour

other gases

We would find it difficult to exist without electricity, but the power stations that supply it cause pollution. Fuel-burning power stations produce waste gases, as shown above. Nuclear power stations don't burn their fuel, but they produce radioactive waste.

- Fuel-burning power stations put carbon dioxide gas into the atmosphere. The carbon dioxide traps the Sun's energy and may be adding to **global warming**.
- Coal-burning power stations also produce sulphur dioxide gas. This causes **acid rain**, which damages stonework. One solution is to burn expensive low-sulphur coal. Another is to fit costly **flue gas desulphurization** (**FGD**) units to the power stations.
- Transporting fuels can cause pollution. For example, there may be a leak from an oil tanker at sea.
- The radioactive waste from nuclear power stations is highly dangerous. It must be carried away and stored safely in sealed containers for many years – in some cases, thousands of years.
- Nuclear accidents are rare. But when they do occur, radioactive gas and dust can be carried thousands of kilometres by winds.

*One effect of acid rain.*

*If a tanker runs aground and leaks oil, the effects on the coast and its wildlife can be devastating.*

## Power from water and wind

Some generators are turned by the force of moving water or wind. Power schemes like this have no fuel costs, and give off no polluting gases. However, they can be expensive to build, and need large areas of land.

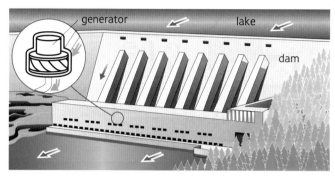

**Hydroelectric power scheme**  *Rivers and rainwater fill up a lake behind a dam. As water rushes down from the dam, it turns turbines which turn generators.*

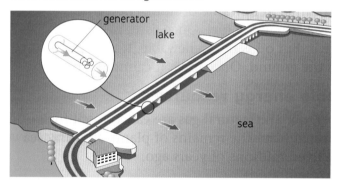

**Tidal power scheme**  *A dam is built across a river where it meets the sea. The lake behind the dam fills when the tide comes in and empties when the tide goes out. The flow of water turns the generators.*

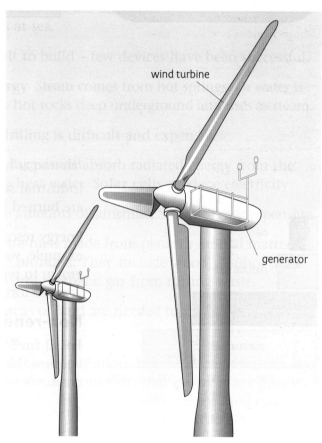

**Wind farm**  *This is a collection of **aerogenerators** – generators driven by giant wind turbines ('windmills').*

## Questions

1 Write down *three* types of power station that do *not* burn fuel.

2 Fuel-burning power stations give off carbon dioxide gas. What problem is caused by putting this gas into the atmosphere?

3 Describe how the generators are turned in a hydroelectric power scheme.

4 What are *aerogenerators*?

5 Coal-burning power stations also produce sulphur dioxide.

a What is the effect of putting this gas into the atmosphere?

b How can the amount of sulphur dioxide be reduced?

6 Nuclear power stations don't add to global warming.

a Why don't they add to global warming?

b Give *two* reasons why especially high safety standards are needed in nuclear power stations.

# 9.13   How the world gets its energy

## Solar panels

These absorb energy radiated from the Sun and use it to heat water.

## Solar cells

These use the energy in sunlight to produce small amounts of electricity.

## The Sun

The Sun radiates energy because of nuclear reactions deep inside it. Its output is equivalent to 400 million billion billion electric hotplates! Just a tiny fraction reaches the Earth.

## Energy in Plants

Plants take in energy from sunlight falling on their leaves. They use it to turn water and carbon dioxide from the air into new growth. Animals eat plants to get the energy stored in them.

## Energy in food

We get energy from the food we eat. The food may be from plants, or from animals which fed on plants.

## Biofuels from plants

Wood is still an important fuel in many countries. When wood is burnt, it releases energy which the tree took in from the Sun. In some countries, sugar cane is grown and fermented to make alcohol. This can be used as a fuel instead of petrol.

## Fossil fuels

Oil, natural gas, and coal are called fossil fuels. They were formed from the remains of plants and tiny sea creatures which lived many millions of years ago. Industrial societies rely on fossil fuels for most of their energy. Many power stations burn fossil fuels.

## Biofuels from waste

Rotting animal and plant waste can give off methane gas (as in natural gas). This can be used as a fuel. Marshes, rubbish tips, and sewage treatment works are all sources of methane. Some waste can also be used directly as fuel by burning it.

## Batteries

Some batteries (for instance car batteries) have to be given energy by charging them with electricity. Others are manufactured from chemicals which already store energy. But energy is needed to produce the chemical in the first place.

## Fuels from oil

Many fuels can be extracted from oil. These include: petrol, diesel fuel, jet fuel, paraffin, central heating oil, bottled gas.

### The Moon

The gravitational pull of the Moon (and to a lesser extent, the Sun) creates gentle bulges in the Earth's oceans. As the Earth rotates, different places have high and low tides as they pass in and out of the bulges. The motion of the tides carries energy with it.

### Tidal energy

In a tidal energy scheme, an estuary is dammed to form an artificial lake.
Incoming tides fill the lake; outgoing tides empty it. The flow of water in and out of the lake turns generators.

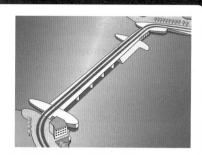

### Nucleus of the atom

Radioactive materials have atoms with unstable nuclei (centres) which break up and release energy. The material gives off the energy slowly as thermal energy. With some nuclei, energy can be released much more quickly by nuclear reactions.

### Nuclear energy

In a reactor, nuclear reactions release energy from the nuclei of uranium atoms.
This produces heat which is used to make steam for driving generators.

### Geothermal energy

Deep underground, the rocks are hotter than they are on the surface. The heat comes from radioactive materials naturally present in the rocks. It can be used to make steam for heating buildings or driving generators.

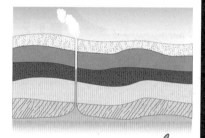

### Weather systems

These are partly driven by energy radiated from the Sun. Heated air rising above the equator causes belts of wind around the Earth. Winds carry water vapour from the oceans and bring rain and snow.

### Wind energy

For centuries, people have been using the power of the wind to move ships, pump water, and grind corn. Today, huge wind turbines are used to turn generators.

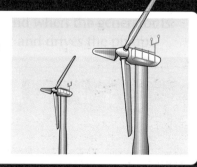

### Wave energy

Waves are caused by the wind (and partly by tides). Waves cause a rapid-up-and-down movement on the surface of the sea. This movement can be used to drive generators.

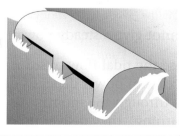

### Hydroelectric energy

An artificial lake forms behind a dam. Water rushing down from this lake is used to turn generators. The lake is kept full by river water which once fell as rain or snow.

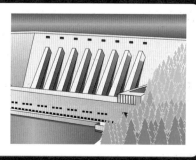

# ESCAPING HEAT

Most houses waste energy. When it is cold outside, the biggest waste of energy is lost heat. This is how the heat escapes from a typical house.

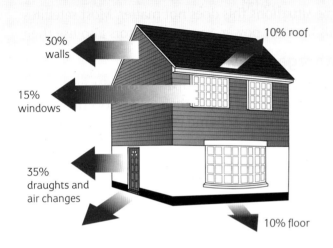

10% roof

30% walls

15% windows

35% draughts and air changes

10% floor

## New air for old

Stopping draughts and air changes saves most on the fuel bills. But it can put your health – and even your life – at risk. If rooms are tightly sealed, any oxygen used up isn't replaced. Also, harmful substances collect in the air.

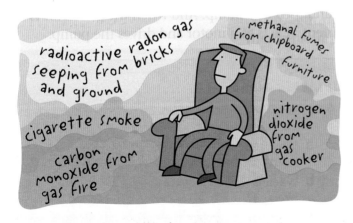

radioactive radon gas seeping from bricks and ground

methanal fumes from chipboard furniture

cigarette smoke

nitrogen dioxide from gas cooker

carbon monoxide from gas fire

A room should have at least one complete change of air per hour. In a draughty house, there may be 15 or more. This is good for clearing the air, but it makes the house expensive to heat.

## U-values

To calculate likely heat losses from a house, architects need to know the **U-values** of different materials. For example:

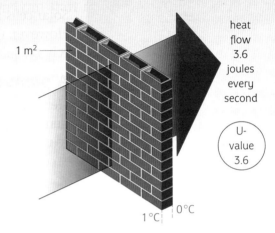

1 m$^2$

heat flow 3.6 joules every second

U-value 3.6

1°C   0°C

A single-brick wall has a U-value of 3.6 W/(m$^2$ °C). This means that a square metre of the wall, with a 1°C temperature difference across it, will conduct heat at the rate of 3.6 joules per second.

The heat flow is greater if:

* the temperature difference is higher.
* the area is greater.
* the wall is thinner.

| U-value | W/(m$^2$ °C) |
|---|---|
| single-brick wall | 3.6 |
| double wall, with air cavity | 1.7 |
| double wall, with insulating fibrewool in cavity | 0.5 |
| glass window, single layer | 5.7 |
| double-glazed window | 2.7 |

The lower the U-value, the better the material is as an insulator.

# Low-energy houses

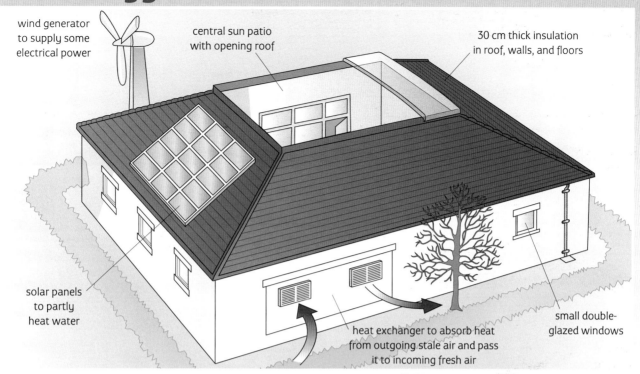

wind generator to supply some electrical power

central sun patio with opening roof

30 cm thick insulation in roof, walls, and floors

solar panels to partly heat water

heat exchanger to absorb heat from outgoing stale air and pass it to incoming fresh air

small double-glazed windows

This is a design for a low-energy house. In winter, the power of a one-bar electric heater is enough to heat the whole house. The house is good for the environment – but, unfortunately, it is far too expensive for most people to buy. Also, there is one way in which it could be improved…

For the same level of insulation, a terraced house like the one on the right wastes less energy than other types. Sandwiched between other buildings, it has a smaller surface area for heat to escape to the outside.

## Talking points

- In cold conditions, most houses waste too much heat.

    ❊ What causes the greatest loss of heat from a house?

    ❊ Why can it be dangerous to stop this loss completely?

- Look at the table of U-values opposite.

    ❊ Which will let most heat escape, a double wall with air cavity or a double-glazed window of the same area?

    ❊ Are houses with small windows likely to lose less heat than those with larger windows? Can you explain your answer?

# WARM to the core COLD risks

In winter, someone's hands and feet may be cold, but they can cope with the harsh conditions outside, provided the temperature of their body's **core** doesn't drop below the normal 37 °C.

If the body loses too much heat, and its core temperature drops more than 2 °C, it stops working properly. The condition is called **hypothermia**.

Old people are at risk from hypothermia if their homes are not heated properly.

Exercise is a particularly good way of keeping warm. That is because the human body isn't very efficient as an 'engine'. For every joule of energy delivered by your muscles, your body must release about 6 joules from your food by 'burning' it. The other 5 joules warm you up!

Young babies also find it difficult to cope with the cold. They don't store as much body heat as adults, so any loss has a bigger effect. And they can't adjust to sudden heat losses because their temperature control system isn't fully developed.

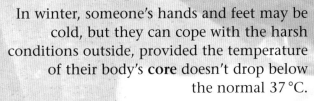

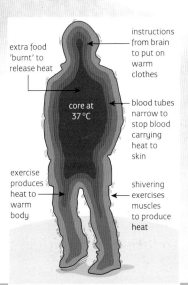

instructions from brain to put on warm clothes

extra food 'burnt' to release heat

core at 37 °C

blood tubes narrow to stop blood carrying heat to skin

exercise produces heat to warm body

shivering exercises muscles to produce heat

*How the body keeps warm.*

# Reducing radiation

These shiny capes help keep marathon runners warm when the race is over.

# Survival at sea

If the windsurfer in the photo gets in the water without an insulating suit, he could be suffering from hypothermia in minutes. In a cold sea, the human body loses heat over 20 times faster than in cold air.

A wet-suit is worn with a layer of water trapped between the suit and the diver's skin. The water is an insulator. More insulation comes from the thousands of tiny nitrogen bubbles trapped in the suit's lining.

# Polar lifestyle

With lots of fur to trap air, and layers of thick fat under the skin for extra insulation, a polar bear has no problems retaining body heat. Even a swim in icy water can seem quite pleasant if there's a chance of catching a meal at the same time.

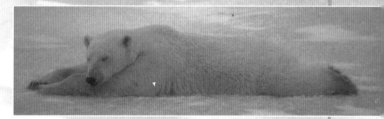

## Talking points

Can you suggest a reason for each of the following?

❄ Exercise warms you up.

❄ Old people are more at risk from hypothermia than younger people.

❄ Marathon runners may put on a shiny cape when the race is over.

❄ The changing room at a swimming pool is kept at a temperature of 25 °C, but the pool itself is kept at 30 °C.

# Power plus

## Guaranteed POWER

Power cuts don't happen very often. But when they do, the results can be serious:

If there is a loss of power in a dairy, two hundred cows will need milking by hand.

A loss of power in an operating theatre might put someone's life at risk.

For emergencies, most large hospitals and farms have stand-by generators. They are driven by engines which run on petrol, diesel, or bottled gas. They start up automatically if there is a mains failure.

## Extra POWER

In Somerset, hens have solved one farmer's electricity supply problems. He saves their droppings in a tank, collects the gas given off, and uses it to run the engine for his generator.

In Florida, the police have collected so many drugs in raids that a power station has been converted to burn them. One tonne of marijuana gives nearly as much heat as three barrels of oil.

In Edmonton, North London, the council has turned one of its incinerators into a power station, using household rubbish as the fuel. The council gets rid of its waste, and keeps costs down by selling its electricity to a power company.

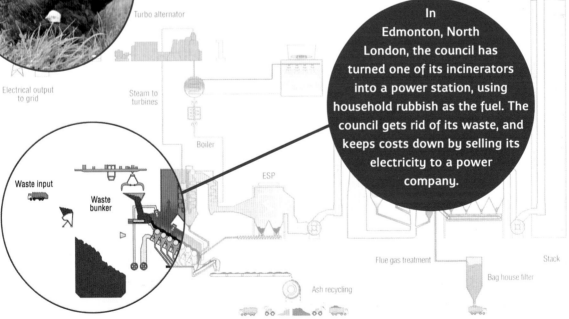

Turbo alternator

Electrical output to grid

Steam to turbines

Boiler

ESP

Waste input

Waste bunker

Flue gas treatment

Stack

Bag house filter

Ash recycling

# Water POWER

The world's first power station was opened in 1881 at Godalming in Surrey. Its generator was driven by a paddle wheel, turned by water flowing from the River Wey. Its output was small and only supplied current for the local street lights. Today's some of the world's largest power stations still use flowing water. They are hydroelectric power stations.

The Hoover Dam, Colorado USA is over 220 metres high. The generators near its base are turned by giant water turbines.

In Sweden, much of the electricity comes from hydroelectric schemes. But plans to build more dams have been dropped because of concerns about environmental damage.

In Sri Lanka, the government wants to build more dams. Unless the country can generate power with its own resources, it will have to import more oil, and that will keep the country poor.

In Egypt, when the Aswan Dam was constructed, and the land behind it flooded, the ancient temple at Abu Simnel had to be cut from the rock and rebuilt on higher ground.

## Talking points

Using the index, or other sources of information, see if you can find out:

- what fuels are normally used in power stations

- what features electric motors and generators have in common.

Electricity supply companies have special departments which look ahead to find out when the most popular TV programmes are going to start and finish. Can you suggest reasons why?

# Electricity

# Module 10

A worker inside a safety cage looks on as 2.5 million volt sparks come from a huge Van de Graaff generator. The sparks are produced when electric charge flows through the air, heats it, and makes it light up. Heating and lighting are just two of electricity's effects, although the results are usually less spectacular than in this experiment.

# Electricity on the move

When you switch on a hairdrier, lamp, or TV, the 'electricity' in the wires is a flow of tiny particles called **electrons**. These are so small that they can pass between the atoms of the wire. They each carry a tiny electric **charge**.

A flow of charge is called a **current**. So a flow of electrons is a current.

When a torch is working, more than 1 million million million electrons flow through its bulb every second!

## Conductors and insulators

Materials that let current pass through are called **conductors**. Materials that do not let current pass through are **insulators**. Here are some examples.

## Questions

1 What word means:
   **a** a flow of charge?
   **b** a material that lets current pass through?
   **c** a material that does not let current pass through?

| Conductors | | Insulators | |
|---|---|---|---|
| *Good* | *Poor* | plastics | glass |
| metals | human body | *for example* | rubber |
| *especially* | water | PVC | |
| silver | air | polythene | |
| copper | | Perspex | |
| aluminium | | | |
| carbon | | | |

In an electric cable like the one on the left, copper wires carry the current. The PVC insulation stops current flowing between the wires, and stops the wires touching anything outside the cable.

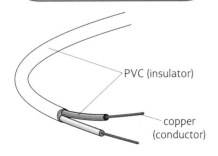

PVC (insulator)

copper (conductor)

*The bulbs on this carnival float get their current from a generator turned by a diesel engine.*

*A cell.*

## Sources of current

Our main sources of current are electric **cells**, **batteries**, and **generators**. For example, mains current comes from huge generators in power stations.

Cells and batteries push out current when chemicals inside them react. Generators push out current when a shaft is turned. In power stations, the generators are often turned by turbines driven round by jets of high-pressure steam from a boiler.

## Using current

A current is a convenient way of delivering energy. Here are some of the ways of using that energy:

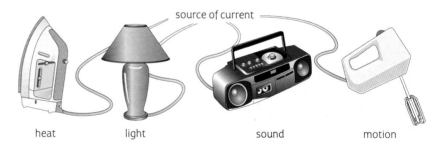

source of current

heat          light          sound          motion

## Questions

**2** Name a material that could be used for making each of the following:

   **a** the wire inside an electric cable.

   **b** the insulation round the outside of the cable.

**3** Write down the name of a device which:

   **a** pushes out a current when chemicals react inside it.

   **b** pushes out a current when a shaft is turned.

**4** Write down:

   **a** two things that get their current from cells or batteries.

   **b** two things that get their current from generators.

**5** Write down:

   **a** two things that use current to produce motion.

   **b** two things that use current to produce heat.

   **c** two things that use current to produce sound.

# Circuits and currents

## A simple circuit

Below, a **cell** has been connected to a bulb and a switch. The complete loop is known as a **circuit**. Electrons are pushed out of the **negative (–) terminal** of the cell, through the bulb and switch, and round to the **positive (+)** terminal. As they pass through the bulb, they heat up a tiny filament (thin wire) so that it glows.

There must be a *complete* circuit for electrons to flow. If there is a break in the circuit, the flow stops, and the bulb goes out. Turning the switch OFF breaks the circuit.

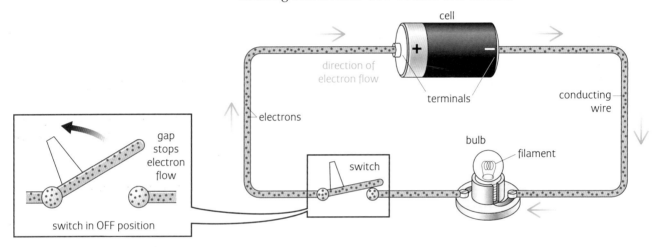

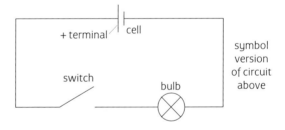

## Circuit symbols

To keep things easy, scientists and electricians draw circuits using special symbols. You can see an example above.

Unfortunately, the standard symbol for a switch looks OFF even though the switch may be ON! So alternative symbols are sometimes used. There is also an alternative symbol for a bulb.

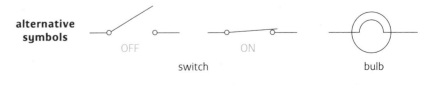

**Questions**

1  Give *two* things that are necessary to make a current flow through a small bulb.

2  What do the following symbols mean?

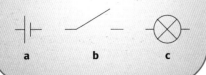

a        b        c

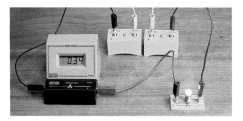

*An ammeter in use.*

ammeter symbol

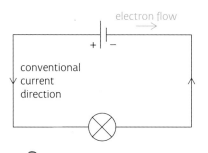

conventional current direction

## Measuring current

Current is measured in **amperes** (A). The higher the current, the greater the flow of charge. In other words, the more electrons pass round the circuit every second.

To measure current, you connect an **ammeter** into the circuit, as shown in the examples below. Fitting the ammeter doesn't affect the current. As far as the circuit is concerned, the ammeter is just like another piece of connecting wire.

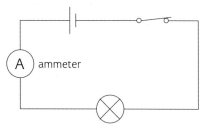

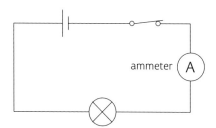

In simple circuits like those above, it doesn't matter where the ammeter goes, because the current is the same all the way round. The same electrons pass through one section after another.

Small currents can be measured in **milliamperes** (mA):

1000 mA = 1 A

So, for example, a current of 0.4 A is 400 mA.

## Current direction

On some circuit diagrams, you may see an arrowhead. This is called the **conventional current direction**. It isn't really a direction of flow. It just shows the direction from positive (+) to negative (–) round the circuit. The electrons actually flow the opposite way.

## Questions

**3** In the circuit on the right, meters X and Y measure current.

  **a** What type of meter are X and Y?

  **b** Would you expect the reading on meter Y to be *more*, *less*, or the *same* as that on meter X?

  If the switch is opened...

  **c** will bulb A stay on or go out?

  **d** will bulb B stay on or go out?

  **e** what will happen to the reading on meter X?

  **f** what will happen to the reading on meter Y?

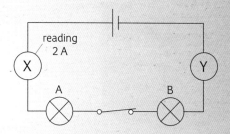

**4** The current through a small torch bulb is 0.2 A. What is this in milliamperes?

**Objectives**

**This spread should help you to**

• explain what 'voltage' tells you about a cell, a battery, or part of a circuit

Cells store energy. When a cell is connected into a circuit, as below, chemical reactions inside the cell push out electrons and *give* them energy. The electrons *lose* this energy when they flow through the bulb. The energy is given off as heat and light.

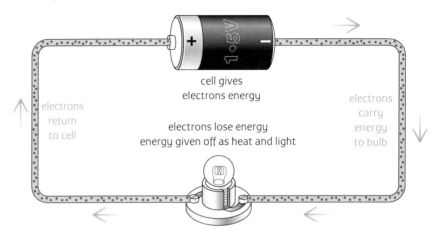

electrons return to cell

cell gives electrons energy

electrons lose energy
energy given off as heat and light

electrons carry energy to bulb

**Did you know?**

**Typical voltages**

Voltage across...

| | |
|---|---|
| ... a cell for a torch | 1.5 V |
| ... a car battery | 12 V |
| ... a mains socket | 230 V |

## Cells and voltage

Cells have a **voltage** marked on the side. The higher the voltage, the more energy each electron is given.

Voltage is also known as **potential difference** (**p.d.**). It is measured in **volts** (V). The voltage of a cell can be measured by connecting a **voltmeter** across its terminals.

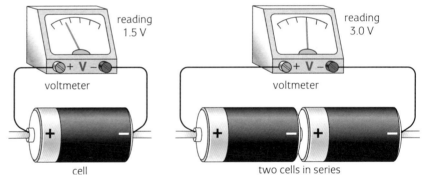

reading 1.5 V

voltmeter

cell

reading 3.0 V

voltmeter

two cells in series

If two identical cells are connected in **series** (in a line), the total voltage across them is twice that across a single cell.

A collection of linked cells is called a **battery**, although the word is commonly used for a single cell as well.

*This 12 volt car battery has six 2 volt cells connected in series, all in the same case.*

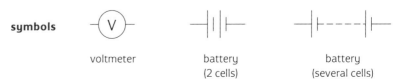

symbols

voltmeter

battery
(2 cells)

battery
(several cells)

## Voltages round a circuit

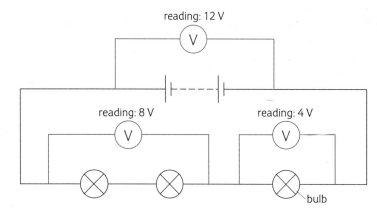

reading: 12 V

reading: 8 V  reading: 4 V

bulb

### Questions

1  How would you draw three cells in series, using symbols?
2  What type of meter would you use to measure p.d.?
3  What single word means the same thing as p.d.?

*Most personal CD players are powered by two 1.5 V cells connected in series.*

Above, a 12 V battery has been connected across three bulbs. The electrons lose some of their energy in the first bulb, some in the second, and the rest in the third.

Connect a voltmeter across any of the bulbs and it shows a reading. The higher the voltage, the more energy each electron loses as it passes through that part of the circuit.

Between them, the bulbs give out all the energy supplied by the battery:

The voltages across the bulbs add up to equal the battery voltage.

Connecting the voltmeters has no effect on the current flowing in the circuit above. As far as the circuit is concerned, the voltmeters might as well not be there.

### Questions

4  The circuit on the right contains a battery and two bulbs.
   a  Which part of the circuit stores energy?
   b  In which parts of the circuit is energy being used?
   c  The battery is made up of three cells. What would you expect the voltage of each cell to be?
   d  What will be the reading on meter **Z**?
   e  If an extra cell is added to the battery, what would you expect the new reading to be on...
   meter **X**?      meter **Y**?      meter **Z**?

5  Look at the circuit at the top of this page. If the meter that reads 8 V was connected across only one bulb instead of two, what would you expect it to read?

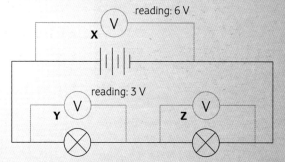

reading: 6 V

**X**

reading: 3 V

**Y**    **Z**

# Resistance

## Objectives

**This spread should help you to**
- calculate resistance
- explain what resistors are

Current passes easily through a piece of copper connecting wire. It doesn't pass so easily through the thin nichrome wire of an electric fire element. The wire has more **resistance**. Energy has to be used to force electrons through it, and heat is given off as a result.

Long wires have more resistance...                    ... than short ones.

Thin wires have more resistance...                    ... than thick ones.

Nichrome wire has
more resistance...                                              ... than copper wire
of the same size.

## Calculating resistance

Resistance is measured in **ohms** (Ω). If a voltage is put across the ends of a wire, a current flows. The resistance of the wire, in ohms, can be calculated using this equation:

## Questions

1  In what unit is resistance measured?
2  What equation is used to calculate resistance?

$$\text{resistance} = \frac{\text{voltage}}{\text{current}}$$

voltage in volts (V)
current in amperes (A)
resistance in ohms (Ω)

For example:

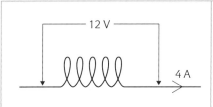

If there is a voltage of 12 V across this piece of nichrome wire, a current of 4 A flows. So:

$$\text{resistance} = \frac{12}{4} = 3\,\Omega$$

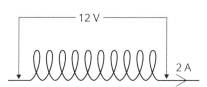

If there is a voltage of 12 V across this piece of nichrome wire, a current of 2 A flows. So:

$$\text{resistance} = \frac{12}{2} = 6\,\Omega$$

So, for any particular voltage:

The *higher* the resistance, the *lower* the current through the wire.

## Heat from resistance

When current flows through a resistance, heat is given off. This idea is used in the filament of a light bulb. It is also used in the heating elements of electric kettles, irons, toasters, and hairdriers.

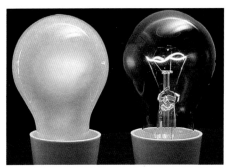

*The filament of a light bulb is made from very thin tungsten wire. Because of its resistance, it gets very hot when a current flows through.*

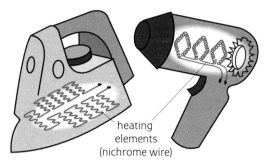

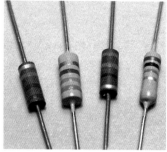

heating
elements
(nichrome wire)

*Heating elements have resistance....*    *...and so do these resistors.*

## Resistors

**Resistors** also give off heat when a current flows through, but that isn't their job. They can be used to reduce current. In electronics circuits, like those in TVs and radios, they are used to keep currents at the right levels so that other parts work properly.

On the left, a **variable resistor** is being used to control the brightness of a bulb. The variable resistor contains a long coil of thin nichrome wire. Sliding the control to the right puts more resistance into the circuit, so the bulb gets dimmer.

Some variable resistors are rotary – you turn the control rather than slide it. Variable resistors like this are used in computer joysticks. They can also be used as volume controls, though most radios and TVs now have press buttons linked to a microchip for this.

*A variable resistor (rotary type).*

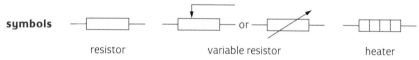

**symbols**        resistor        variable resistor    or        heater

## Questions

**3** On this page, there is a diagram of a circuit containing a variable resistor.

  **a** How is a variable resistor different from an ordinary resistor?

  **b** If, in the diagram, the variable resistor's control is slid to the left, what effect will this have? Give a reason for your answer.

  **c** Redraw the diagram so that only circuit symbols are used.

**4** Why is the heating element in a hairdrier made of thin nichrome wire rather than thick copper wire?

**5** Copy and complete the table below, using the resistance equation to work out the missing values:

|  | Resistor A | Resistor B | Resistor C |
|---|---|---|---|
| voltage across resistor in V | 8 | 6 | 2 |
| current through resistor in A | 2 | 4 | 5 |
| resistance in Ω |  |  |  |

# More about resistance

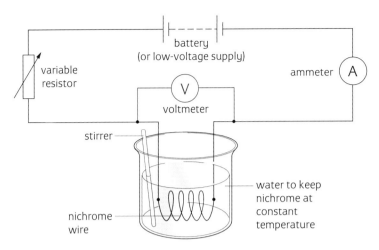

| Voltage in V | Current in A | Resistance in Ω $= \dfrac{\text{voltage}}{\text{current}}$ |
|:---:|:---:|:---:|
| 3.0 | 1.0 | 3.0 |
| 6.0 | 2.0 | 3.0 |
| 9.0 | 3.0 | 3.0 |
| 12.0 | 4.0 | 3.0 |

With the circuit above, you can find how the current through a conductor depends on the voltage across it. Here, the conductor is a coil of nichrome wire, kept at a steady temperature. The table on the left gives some typical results. They show that:

- If the voltage doubles, the current doubles, and so on.
- The resistance across the nichrome wire keeps the same value, 3 Ω in this case.

If a material has the same resistance for all currents, then scientists say that it obeys **Ohm's law**. All metals obey Ohm's law – provided that their temperature doesn't change.

The resistance of a metal increases with temperature. However, the increase is small, unless the temperature rise is very large.

## Resistance components

Some of the **components** (parts) used in circuits are designed to have a resistance which can vary:

| Component | Thermistor | Light-dependent resistor | Diode |
|---|---|---|---|
| Symbol | | | |
| Resistance | High resistance when cold, low resistance when hot. | High resistance in the dark, low resistance in the light. | Very high resistance in one direction, low resistance in other. |
| Examples of use | In electronic circuits which detect temperature change – for example, in fire alarms or thermometers. | In electronic circuits which switch on lights automatically. | Lets current flow in one direction only. Used in power adaptors and electronic equipment. |

## Current–voltage graphs

With readings taken using a circuit like the one on the opposite page, current–voltage graphs can be produced for different components. Here are some examples:

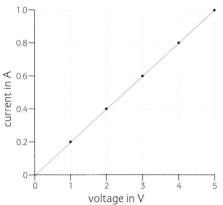

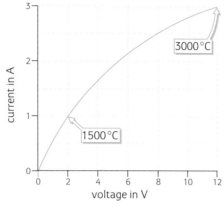

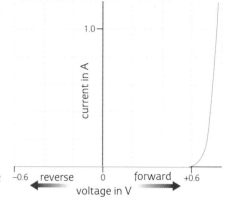

*A metal resistor at a steady temperature (for instance, the nichrome wire on the opposite page). The graph is a straight line through the origin. Voltage ÷ current is the same at all points. In other words, the resistance doesn't change.*

*A tungsten filament (in a bulb). As the current increases, the temperature rises and the resistance goes up.*
*Voltage ÷ current is not the same at all points. The current is not proportional to the voltage.*

*A diode. The current is not proportional to the voltage. And if the voltage is reversed (by connecting the diode the other way round), the current is almost zero. In effect, the diode 'blocks' current in the reverse direction.*

## Adding resistances

These resistors in series...

3 Ω    6 Ω

... have the same effect as this resistance.

9 Ω

If you connect more and more resistors in series, the total resistance is increased:

If resistances are connected in series:
   total resistance = sum of separate resistances

For example, on the left, resistances of 3 Ω and 6 Ω in series have a total resistance of 9 Ω.

## Questions

**1** Name a component which:

  **a** has a resistance that falls as its temperature rises.

  **b** lets current flow through it in one direction only.

**2** Look at the graph for the tungsten filament at the top of this page.

  **a** What is the current through the filament when the voltage across it is 2 V?

  **b** What is the current through the filament when the voltage across it is 12 V?

  **c** What is the resistance of the filament at 1500 °C?

  **d** What is the resistance of the filament at 3000 °C?

**3** A piece of nichrome wire is kept at a steady temperature. Different voltages are put across the ends of the wire, and the current measured each time. Copy the table below and fill in the missing values:

| Voltage in V | Current in A | Resistance in Ω |
|---|---|---|
| 8 | 2 | |
| 4 | | |
| 2 | | |

# Series and parallel circuits

The bulbs above have to get their power from the same supply. There are two ways of connecting bulbs or resistors together. The circuits below show the differences between them.

These bulbs are connected in **series**.

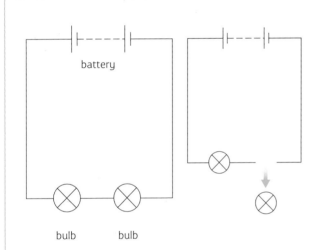

battery

bulb  bulb

- The bulbs share the voltage from the battery, so each glows dimly.
- If one bulb is removed, the other goes out because the circuit is broken.

These bulbs are connected in **parallel**.

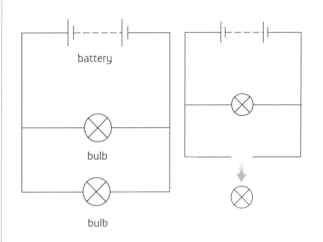

battery

bulb

bulb

- Each bulb gets the full voltage from the battery, so each glows brightly.
- If one bulb is removed, the other keeps working because it is still part of an unbroken circuit.

**Questions**

**1** Some bulbs are to be powered by the same battery. Give *two* advantages of connecting the bulbs in parallel rather than in series.

If two or more bulbs have to be powered by one battery (or power supply), they are usually connected in parallel. Each bulb gets the full battery voltage. Also, each can be switched on or off by itself.

## Basic circuit rules

The examples at the top of the next page show the basic rules for series and parallel circuits. But whatever the arrangement, resistance = voltage ÷ current *always* applies to *every* resistance. Check it for yourself on the resistors in the diagrams!

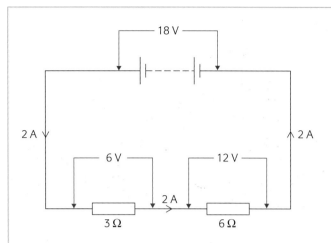

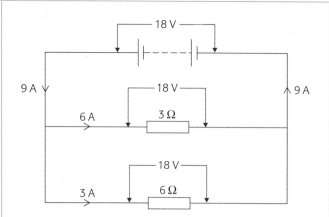

When a battery is connected across resistors (or other components) in **series**:

- each resistor has the same current through it.
- the resistors share the battery voltage. So the voltages across them add up to equal the battery voltage.

When a battery is connected across resistors (or other components) in **parallel**:

- each resistor gets the full battery voltage.
- the resistors share the current from the battery. So the currents through them add up to equal the current from the battery.

## Cell arrangements

Here are some examples of linked cells:

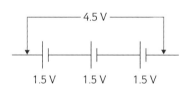

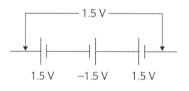

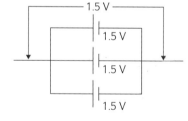

*Cells in series: you add up their voltages to find the total voltage.*

*One cell is the wrong way round, so it cancels out one of the others.*

*The voltage across parallel cells is the same as from a single cell.*

## Questions

*These questions are about the circuit on the right.*

**2** Will each of the bulbs A and B be ON or OFF if:

   **a** switch $S_1$ only is opened?

   **b** switch $S_2$ only is opened?

**3** Bulbs A and B are identical. If both switches are closed:

   **a** what is the voltage across bulb A?

   **b** what is the current through bulb B?

   **c** what is the current through the battery?

**4** The battery is made up of four cells.

   **a** What is the voltage of each cell?

   **b** What would the battery voltage be if one of the cells were connected the wrong way round?

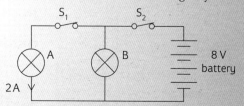

# Solving circuits

## Objectives

**This spread should help you to**

- calculate voltage, current, and resistance values in different parts of a circuit

Sound and lighting equipment like that above contains hundreds of circuits. To produce such circuits, electrical engineers need to understand the link between voltage, current, and resistance.

## Resistance–voltage–current equations

If you know the voltage across a resistor, and the current through it, you calculate the resistance with this equation:

$$\text{resistance} = \frac{\text{voltage}}{\text{current}}$$

voltage in volts (V)
current in amperes (A)
resistance in ohms (Ω)

The equation can be rearranged in two ways:

$$\text{voltage} = \text{current} \times \text{resistance} \qquad \text{current} = \frac{\text{voltage}}{\text{resistance}}$$

These are useful if you already know the resistance, but need to find the voltage or current.

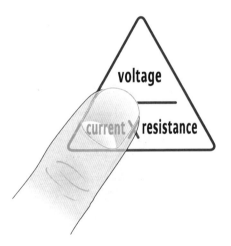

*Cover 'current' if you want the equation for current. It works for voltage and resistance as well.*

The triangle on the left gives all three versions of the equation.

## Circuit problems

**Example 1** A current of 2A flows through a 3Ω resistor. What is the voltage across the resistor?

In this case:

current = 2A, resistance = 3Ω, and voltage is to be found. So, choose the equation starting voltage = ...

$$\text{voltage} = \text{current} \times \text{resistance} = 2 \times 3 = 6\,\text{V}$$

So, the voltage across the resistor is 6V.

## Questions

**1** A current of 2A flows through a 6Ω resistor. What is the voltage across the resistor?

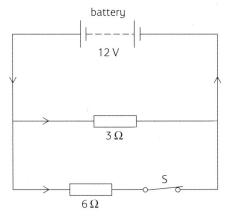

battery
12 V
3 Ω
6 Ω
S

**Example 2** In the circuit on the left, what is the current through: **a** the 3Ω resistor? **b** the 6Ω resistor? **c** the battery?

**a** The 3Ω resistor has the full battery voltage across it.
So, in this case:
voltage = 12 V, resistance = 3Ω, and current is to be found.
So, choose the equation starting current = ...

$$\text{current} = \frac{\text{voltage}}{\text{resistance}} = \frac{12}{3} = 4\,A$$

So, the current through the 3Ω resistor is 4 A.

**b** The 6 Ω resistor also has the full battery voltage across it.
So you solve the problem using the same method as above.
The current through the 6Ω resistor is 2 A.

**c** The battery has to supply current for *both* resistors. So:

| current through battery | = | current through 6Ω resistor | + | current through 3Ω resistor | |
|---|---|---|---|---|---|
| | = | 4 A | + | 2 A | = 6 A |

So, the current through the battery is 6 A.

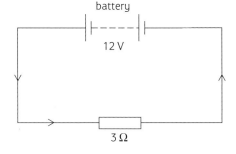

battery
12 V
3 Ω

**Example 3** In example **2** above, what is the current through the battery if the switch S is opened?

This is easier than it looks! If switch S is opened, there is no current through the 6Ω resistor, and the circuit behaves just like the one on the left. The 3Ω resistor still has a current of 4 A through it. So, the current through the battery is 4 A.

## Questions

**2** In each of the following, the resistance, voltage, or current needs to be calculated. Find the missing value:

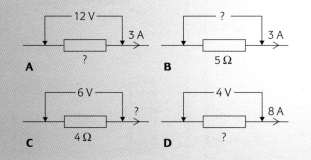

A   12 V   3 A   ?

B   ?   3 A   5 Ω

C   6 V   4 Ω   ?

D   4 V   8 A   ?

**3** In the circuit below, what is the current through:
**a** the 2Ω resistor?   **b** the 4Ω resistor?
**c** the battery?

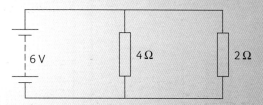

6 V   4 Ω   2 Ω

**4** In the circuit above, if the resistors were connected in series and not parallel, what would the current through each be?

# Magnets and fields

**This spread should help you to**

- describe how magnetic poles push and pull on each other
- describe the magnetic field around a bar magnet

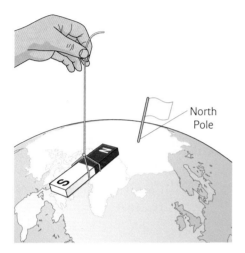

*A suspended bar magnet will turn so that it points roughly north–south.*

## Poles of a magnet

If a small bar magnet is dipped into iron filings, the filings cling to its ends, as shown on the right. The magnetic forces seem to come from two points, called the **poles** of the magnet.

The Earth pulls on the poles of a magnet. If a bar magnet is suspended, as on the left, it turns until it lies roughly north–south. Because of this effect, the two poles of a magnet are called:

- the north-seeking pole (or N pole for short)
- the south-seeking pole (or S pole for short)

If the ends of similar magnets are brought together, as below:

Like poles repel. Unlike poles attract.
The closer the poles, the greater the force between them.

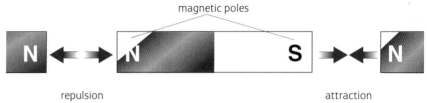

repulsion                                                      attraction

## Permanent and temporary magnets

Pieces of iron and steel *become* magnets if placed near a magnet. The magnet **induces** magnetism in the two metals. It attracts them because the poles nearest each other are different.

When the pieces of metal are pulled away, the steel keeps its magnetism, but the iron does not. The steel has become a **permanent magnet**. The iron was only a **temporary magnet**.

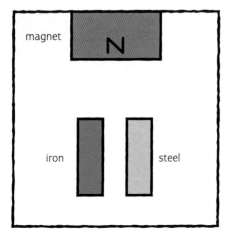

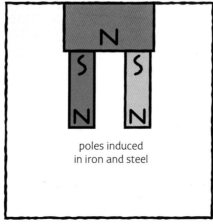

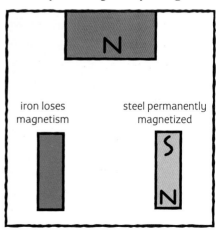

*Iron filings are attracted to the poles of a magnet.*

Materials which can be magnetized and are attracted to magnets are called **magnetic materials**. All strongly magnetic materials contain iron, nickel, or cobalt. For example, steel is mainly iron.

## Field around a magnet

A magnet has a **magnetic field** in the space around it. In this space, there are forces on any magnetic material there.

You can study the field using a small **compass**, as below. The 'needle' is a tiny magnet which is free to turn on its spindle. The forces from the poles of the magnet make it line up with the field.

The Earth is a weak magnet. Its field will turn a compass needle – or any suspended magnet – so that it points roughly north–south.

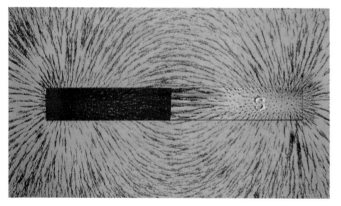

*What happens when iron filings are sprinkled onto a piece of acetate over a bar magnet. The filings have become tiny magnets, pulled into position by forces from the poles of the magnet. Their pattern shows what the **magnetic field** around the magnet is like.*

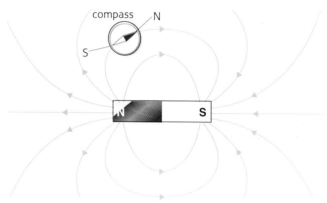

*The field around a magnet can be shown using magnetic **field lines**. These run from the N pole to the S pole of the magnet. They show the direction in which the N end of a compass needle would point. The magnetic field is strongest where the field lines are closest together.*

## Questions

**1** Why are the poles of a magnet called N and S?

**2** What type of magnetic pole:

   **a** attracts an N pole?   **b** repels an S pole?

**3** How can you show that there is a field around a magnet?

**4** In the diagram on the right, pieces of iron and steel are being attracted to the end of a magnet.

   **a** Copy the diagram. Draw in any magnetic poles on the iron and steel.

   **b** If the lower ends of the iron and steel start to move, which way will they move, and why?

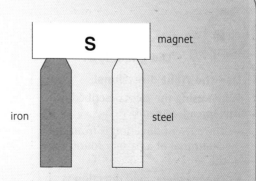

   **c** What happens to each of the metals when it is taken away from the magnet?

# Electromagnets

## Objectives

**This spread should help you to**

- explain how electromagnets work
- describe some uses of electromagnets

An **electromagnet** can do all the things that an ordinary magnet can do, but you can switch it on and off. The one in the photograph above is being used to pick up scrap iron and then drop it.

The diagram below shows a simple electromagnet:

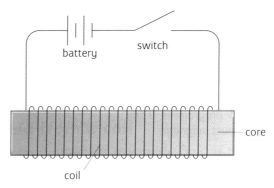

An electromagnet has these parts:

A **coil** made from several hundred turns of insulated copper wire. The more turns there are, the stronger the magnetic field.

A **battery** to supply current. The higher the current, the stronger the magnetic field. If you reverse the current, this reverses the direction of the field.

A **core** made from iron or Mumetal. This makes the field about a thousand times stronger than the coil by itself. Its magnetism dies away as soon as the current is switched off. (Steel would not be suitable as a core because it would stay magnetized.)

The devices on the next page contain electromagnets.

## Questions

1 Why should the core of an electromagnet be made of iron rather than steel?

2 Describe *two* changes you could make to give an electromagnet a stronger pull.

3 What change would you have to make to reverse the direction of the magnetic field from an electromagnet?

## The magnetic relay

With a relay, a small switch with thin wires can be used to turn on the current in a much more powerful circuit – for example, one with a large electric motor in it:

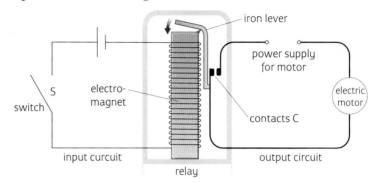

*With a relay, a small switch can be used to turn on a powerful starter motor.*

When you close switch S in the input circuit, a current flows through the electromagnet, and pulls the iron lever towards it, closing contacts C. So current flows through the motor.

## The circuit breaker

A circuit breaker cuts off the current in a circuit if this gets too high. It has the same effect as a fuse but, unlike a fuse, can be reset (turned ON again) after it has tripped (turned OFF).

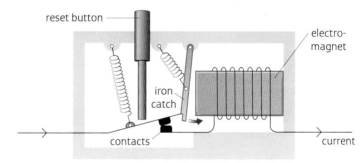

*Some houses have circuit breakers in the 'fuse box', rather than fuses.*

The current flows through two contacts and an electromagnet. If it gets too high, the pull of the electromagnet becomes strong enough to release the iron catch, so the contacts open and stop the current. Pressing the reset button closes them again.

## Questions

**4** In the diagram at the top of the page, an electric motor is controlled by a switch connected to a relay.

  **a** What is the advantage of using a relay, rather than a switch in the motor circuit itself?

  **b** Why does the motor start when switch S is closed?

**5** The diagram above shows a circuit breaker.

  **a** What is the purpose of the circuit breaker?

  **b** What advantage does a circuit breaker have compared with a fuse?

  **c** How do you think the performance of the circuit breaker would be affected if the coil of the electromagnet had more turns?

# Magnets, motion, and motors (1)

## Objectives

**This spread should help you to**
- describe how there is a force on a current in a magnetic field
- give some uses of this force

Magnets don't only push and pull on other magnets and magnetic materials. Their fields also have an effect on an electric current. This idea is used in electric motors, loudspeakers, and meters.

In the diagram below left, a wire has been placed between the poles of a magnet. When a current flows through the wire, there is an upward force on it.

The force becomes stronger if you do the following:

- Increase the current.
- Use a stronger magnet.
- Increase the length of wire in the field.

If you reverse either the current or the field, the force is reversed. If the wire is in line with the field, there isn't any force at all.

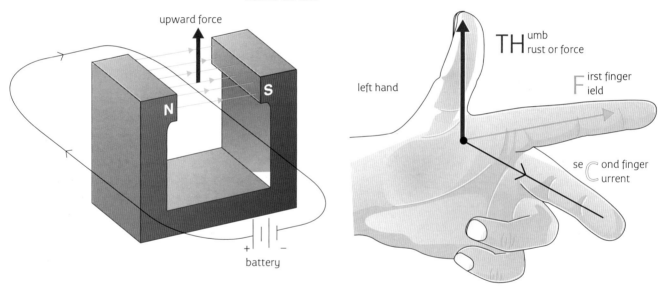

*Fleming's left-hand rule.*

## Fleming's left-hand rule

This is a rule for working out the direction of the force when the current is at right-angles to the magnetic field.

The rule is shown above. It works like this:

Hold the thumb and first two fingers of your left hand at right-angles. If you point your fingers as shown above, your thumb gives the direction of the force.

When you use the rule, remember these points:

- The current direction is from + to –.
- The field lines run from N to S.

## Questions

1 In the diagram above, what would happen if:

  **a** the current was increased?

  **b** the direction of the current was reversed?

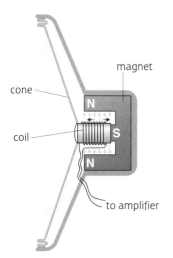

A moving-coil loudspeaker.

## Moving-coil loudspeaker

In the loudspeaker on the left, the magnet is specially shaped so that the wire of the coil is at right-angles to its field. The coil can move in and out. It is attached to a cone made of stiff paper or plastic.

The loudspeaker is connected to an amplifier which gives out an alternating current. This flows backwards and forwards through the wire, causing a force which pushes the coil in and out. So the cone vibrates. And as it vibrates, it gives out sound waves.

## Turning effect on a coil

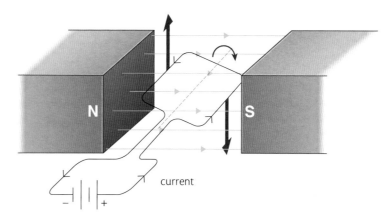

The coil above lies between the poles of a magnet. The current flows in opposite directions along the two sides of the coil. So one side is pushed *up* and the other side is pushed *down*. In other words, there is a turning effect on the coil. With more turns on the coil, the turning effect is stronger. The turning effect is used in electric motors and some meters.

The needle of this meter is moved by a coil which turns in a magnetic field when a current flows through it.

## Questions

2   In the diagram on the right, there is a force on the wire.
   **a** Give *two* ways in which the force could be increased.
   **b** Give *two* ways in which the direction of the force could be reversed.

3   Explain why the cone of a loudspeaker vibrates if alternating current is passed through its coil.

4   The diagram above shows a current-carrying coil in a magnetic field. What difference would it make if:
   **a** there were more turns of wire in the coil?
   **b** the direction of the current were reversed?

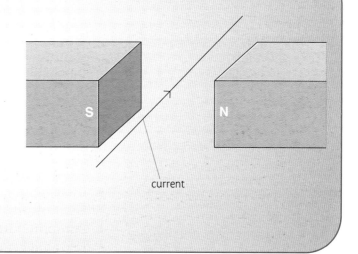

Magnets, motion, and motors (2)

## A simple d.c. motor

The motor below runs on direct current (d.c.), the 'one-way' current that flows from a battery. It uses the idea that a magnetic field can have a turning effect on a coil with a current in it.

The coil is made of insulated copper wire. It is free to rotate between the poles of the magnet. The **commutator**, or split ring, is fixed to the coil and rotates with it. The **brushes** are two contacts which rub against the commutator and keep the coil connected to the battery. They are usually made of carbon.

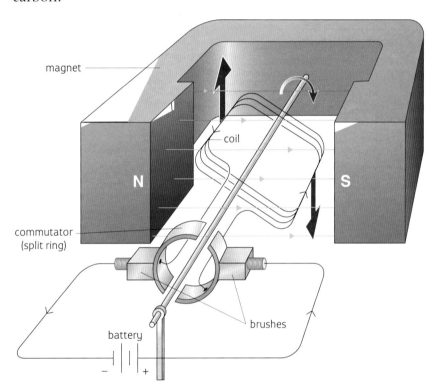

magnet

coil

N

S

commutator
(split ring)

brushes

battery

The two forces above can't pull the coil beyond the vertical position, because they are then pointing the wrong way. The commutator solves this problem with a clever trick: as the coil shoots past the vertical, the commutator *reverses* the current direction. Now the forces point the other way, so the coil is pulled round another half turn... and so on. In this way, the coil keeps rotating.

For a stronger turning effect on the coil, you can:

- Increase the current.
- Use a stronger magnet.
- Put more turns on the coil.
- Use a bigger coil.

**Questions**

1 Which part(s) of an electric motor:

**a** connect the power supply to the split ring and coil?

**b** changes the current direction every half turn?

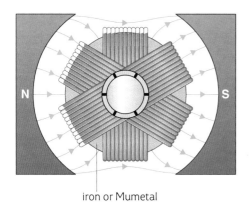

*Practical motors have several coils, wound on iron or Mumetal.*

## Practical motors

Practical motors have several coils set at different angles, each with their own pair of commutator segments (pieces), as shown on the left. The coils are wound on iron or Mumetal to guide the field. These features give smoother running and a greater turning effect.

Some motors use electromagnets rather than permanent magnets. This means that they can run on alternating current (a.c.). As the current flows backwards and forwards through the coil, the field from the electromagnet changes direction to match it, so the turning effect is always the same way. The mains motors in drills and food mixers work like this.

The motors in CD players and in some industrial machines don't have commutators and moving coils. They work on a different principle: the forces are generated by a changing magnetic field.

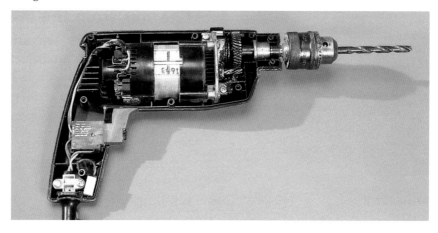

*In this electric drill, the motor is at the right-hand end. Note the commutator segments and the electromagnet.*

## Questions

**2** On the right, there is an end view of the coil in a simple electric motor.

   **a** Why is there an upward force on one side of the coil, but a downward force on the other?

   **b** Give *two* ways in which the turning effect on the coil could be increased.

   **c** Describe *two* things you could change in order to make the motor run backwards.

**3** What is the advantage of using an electromagnet in an electric motor, rather than a permanent magnet?

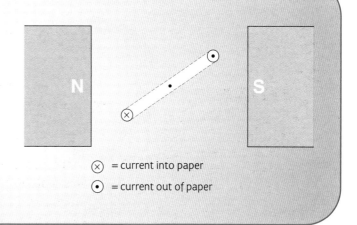

⊗ = current into paper

⊙ = current out of paper

# Electric charge

Charge makes cling-film stick to your hands, and dust stick to a TV screen. It causes crackles and sparks when you comb your hair. It can even make your hair stand on end:

*This person has been charged up. Her hairs all carry the same type of charge, so they repel each other (see opposite page).*

## Charges from the atom

Cling-film, combs, hair, and all other materials are made from atoms. Atoms all have electric charges inside them. In the centre of each atom there is a **nucleus**. This has **positive** (+) **charge**. Around the nucleus, there are electrons, with **negative** (–) **charge**.

Normally, atoms have equal amounts of negative and positive charge, so these cancel out. But electrons don't always stay attached to atoms. For example, they can be removed by rubbing.

## Charging by rubbing

Insulators such as polythene and acetate can become charged when rubbed. People say that they have 'static electricity' on them.

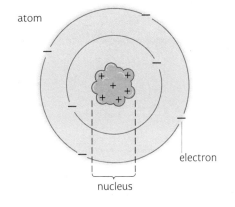

atom

electron

nucleus

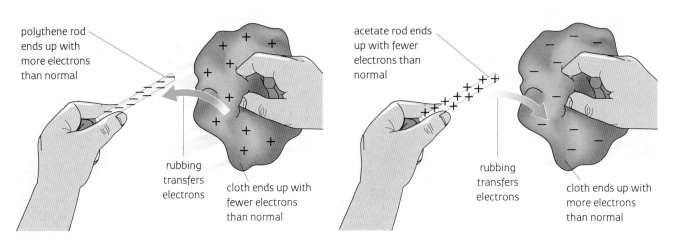

polythene rod ends up with more electrons than normal

rubbing transfers electrons

cloth ends up with fewer electrons than normal

acetate rod ends up with fewer electrons than normal

rubbing transfers electrons

cloth ends up with more electrons than normal

Questions

1 There are two different types of charge. What are they called?

2 A polythene comb becomes charged if you pull it through your hair. Where does the charge come from?

The diagrams on the previous page show what happens when polythene and acetate rods are rubbed with a woollen cloth:

When the polythene rod is rubbed, it pulls electrons from the cloth. So, overall, it ends up negatively (–) charged. The cloth is left positively (+) charged. When the acetate rod is rubbed, the effect is opposite: the cloth pulls electrons from the acetate.

The rubbing action doesn't make electric charge. It just separates charges already there. It works with insulators because, once the charges are separated, they tend to stay where they are.

## Forces between charges

If charged rods are held close, there are forces between them:

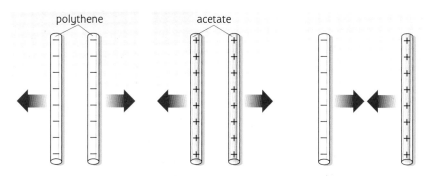

Like charges repel. Unlike charges attract.

A charged object will also attract an *uncharged* one. That is why dust is attracted to the charged screen of a TV. Being uncharged, the dust has equal amounts of + and –, so it feels attraction and repulsion. But the attracted charges are pulled slightly closer than the repelled ones, so the force on them is stronger.

Questions

3 Say whether the things below will attract each other, repel each other, or do neither:

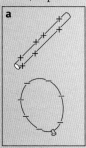 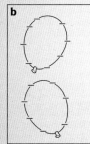 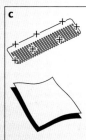

4 A balloon becomes negatively charged when rubbed against someone's sleeve.

   a How does it becomes charged?

   b Why will it then stick to a wall?

# More about charge

Like charges repel, unlike charges attract, and charged objects attract uncharged ones. This spread looks at some effects of these forces.

## Earthing

If enough charge builds up on something, electrons may be pulled through the air and cause sparks. This can be dangerous. To prevent charge building up, objects can be **earthed**: they can be connected to the ground by a conductor so that unwanted charge flows away.

*An aircraft and its tanker must be earthed during refuelling, otherwise charge might build up as the fuel 'rubs' along the pipe. One spark could be enough to ignite the fuel vapour.*

## Photocopiers

Photocopiers also use electric charge, but the charge comes from a power supply rather than from rubbing. Below, you can see the main stages in making a photocopy of a page with a large 'H' on it:

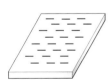 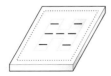  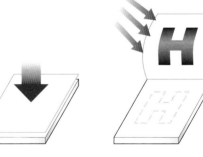

*Inside the photocopier, a light-sensitive plate (or drum) is given a negative charge.*

*An image of the page is projected onto the plate. The bright areas lose their charge but the dark areas keep it.*

*Powdered ink (called **toner**) is attracted to the charged (dark) areas.*

*A blank sheet of paper is pressed against the plate. It picks up powdered ink.*

*The paper is heated so that the powdered ink melts and sticks to it. The result is a copy of the original page.*

## Inkjet printers

An inkjet printer works by squirting tiny droplets of ink at the paper. Each produces a dot. By printing lots of dots, whole letters are formed. But to do this, the printer must control where the droplets go. It uses the force between charges to do this:

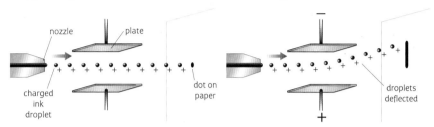

*Ink droplets are charged up as they are forced out of a very narrow nozzle. The droplets pass between two metal plates. If a voltage is put across the plates, they become charged. The charged droplets are attracted to the top plate and repelled by the bottom one, so they are deflected (bent) upwards.*

## Ions on the move

If an atom gains or loses electrons, it becomes charged. A charged atom (or group of atoms) is called an **ion**.

*shapes are simplified and colours are false*

Salty water (water with sodium chloride dissolved in it) contains ions, including those above. In the experiment on the left, a voltage has been put across the liquid. The negative ions are pulled to the **positive electrode** (+ plate), where chlorine gas is given off. The positive ions are pulled to the **negative electrode**, where hydrogen gas is given off. 'Splitting' chemical compounds in this way is called **electrolysis**. The liquid is conducting a current. However, the current is a flow of ions rather than a flow of electrons.

*An inkjet printer.*

## Questions

**1** The build-up of electric charge can be dangerous.
   **a** Give one example of this.
   **b** Describe how the problem can be overcome.

**2 a** In the diagram on the right, what will happen to the droplets as they pass between the plates?
   **b** What difference would it make if the droplets were positively charged instead of negative?

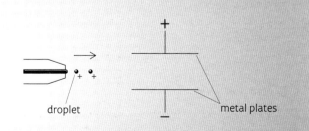

**3** What are *ions*?

**4** Why can salty water conduct a current?

# Mains electricity

When you plug in a kettle, you are connecting it into a circuit. The power comes from a generator in a power station. In the UK, the **supply voltage** for mains sockets and other household circuits is 230 V.

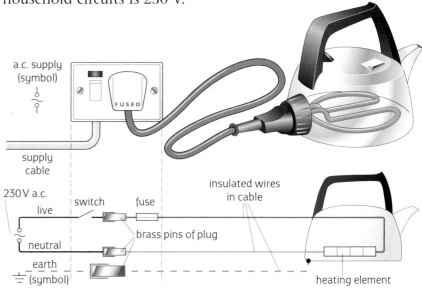

Mains current is **alternating current (a.c.)**. It flows backwards, forwards, backwards, forwards, and so on many times per second.

**Live wire** This goes +, −, +, −, +, −... making the current flow backwards and forwards through the circuit.

**Neutral wire** This completes the circuit. It is at zero voltage.

**Switch** This must be fitted in the live wire so that none of the wire in the flex is still live when you switch off.

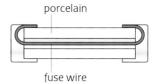

*A cartridge fuse.*

**Fuse** This is a thin piece of wire which heats up and 'blows' (melts) if the current is too high. It breaks the circuit before anything can overheat and catch fire. Like the switch, it must be in the live wire.

**Earth wire** This is a safety wire. It connects the metal casing of the kettle to earth and stops it becoming live. For example, if the live wire comes loose and touches the casing, a current immediately flows to earth and blows the fuse. So the kettle is then safe to touch.

**Did you know?**

When wiring a plug, be sure to check the following:

- The wires are connected to the correct terminals, using the colour code shown on the right.
- The cable is held by the grip.
- The right fuse is fitted (see below right).

If the fuse blows:

- Switch off at the socket and pull out the plug.
- Don't fit a new fuse until the fault has been put right.

# Three-pin plugs

Plugs are a safe and simple way of connecting appliances to the mains. In the UK, three-pin plugs are used. They have a fuse inside them:

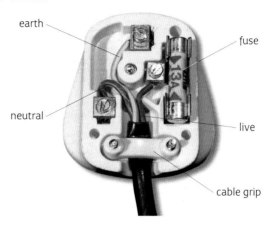

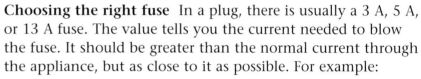

**Choosing the right fuse**  In a plug, there is usually a 3 A, 5 A, or 13 A fuse. The value tells you the current needed to blow the fuse. It should be greater than the normal current through the appliance, but as close to it as possible. For example:

If an electric toaster takes a current of 4 A, it needs a 5 A fuse. It would work with a 13 A fuse, but might not be safe. If something went wrong, its circuits might overheat and catch fire without blowing the fuse.

# Double insulation

The table lamp on the left has a plastic base. This gives it an extra layer of insulation, so it does not need an earth wire. Radios and TVs also have **double insulation** like this, with no earth wire.

*This lamp has double insulation, so it does not need an earth wire.*

## Questions

**6** *live   neutral   earth*   Which of these wires:

  **a** has brown insulation?

  **b** is a safety wire?

  **c** goes alternately + and −?

  **d** has a blue covering?

**7**

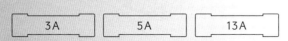

  **a** Which of the above fuses would you choose for a fan heater taking a current of 10 A?

  **b** Which fuse would you choose for a food mixer taking a current of 2 A?

  **c** Why would you *not* use a 13 A fuse for the food mixer in part **b**?

**8** The circuit below has been wrongly wired.

  **a** If the bulb is taken out of its socket, the circuit isn't safe. Explain why not.

  **b** Redraw the circuit, correctly wired.

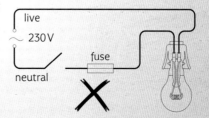

### Objectives

**This spread should help you to**
- explain what 'power' means
- calculate electrical power

The stereo systems above use energy to produce sound. But hers has more **power** than his. It uses more energy every second.

Energy is measured in **joules** (J).

Power is measured in watts (W). A power of 1 watt means that energy is being used at the rate of 1 joule every second.

So a 100 W bulb uses energy at the rate of 100 J every second. It takes 100 J of energy from the mains every second.

Electrical appliances used around the house usually have a power marked on them. You can see some examples below. Sometimes, the power is marked in **kilowatts** (kW):

$$1\,kW = 1000\,W$$

### Questions

1 In what unit is power measured?

2 If a hairdrier has '1.6 kW' marked on it, what is this in watts?

kettle
2300 W

colour TV
115 W

stereo player
92 W

toaster
690 W

drill
460 W

personal stereo
1 W

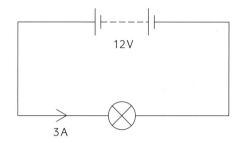

## Calculating electrical power

In circuits, power can be calculated like this:

$$\text{power} = \text{voltage} \times \text{current}$$

power in watts (W)
voltage in volts (V)
current in amperes (A)

For example, the bulb on the left has 12 V across it and a current of 3 A through it. So:

power of bulb = $12 \times 3 = 36\,\text{W}$

## More equations

The power equation above can be rearranged in two ways:

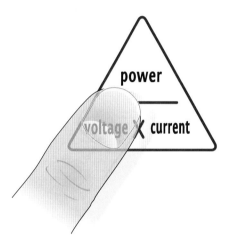

$$\text{current} = \frac{\text{power}}{\text{voltage}} \quad \text{and} \quad \text{voltage} = \frac{\text{power}}{\text{current}}$$

These are useful if you know the power of something, but want to find the voltage or current. The triangle on the left gives all three versions of the equation.

**Example**  A kettle has a power of 2.3 kW. What current does it take from the 230 V mains?

First, change the power into watts: 2.3 kW = 2300 W
Next, use the equation starting current =...

$$\text{current} = \frac{\text{power}}{\text{voltage}} = \frac{2300}{230} = 10\,\text{A}$$

So, the current through the kettle is 10 A.

## Questions

**3** You will find the three appliances below in the pictures showing typical powers on the opposite page. Calculate the power of each one, then work out what they are.

| Mains voltage: 230 V | | |
|---|---|---|
| **A** | **B** | **C** |
| current: 2 A | current: 3 A | current: 0.4 A |

**4** There are four appliances listed on the right.

  **a** What is the power of each appliance in kW?

**b** What current is taken by each appliance?

**c** If you can choose between a 3 A or 13 A fuse, which type would you fit in the plug for each appliance? (Remember: the fuse value should be greater than the normal current, but as close to it as possible.)

| Mains voltage: 230 V | | **Power** |
|---|---|---|
| A | drill | 460 W |
| B | heater | 1150 W |
| C | travel iron | 920 W |
| D | cassette recorder | 23 W |

# More about the mains

## Objectives

**This spread should help you to**

- describe how household circuits are connected
- explain the difference between a.c. and d.c.

## Connecting in parallel

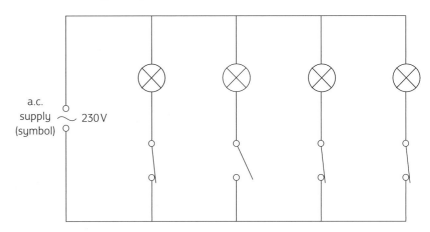

If you need to run four bulbs from the same power supply, then connecting them in parallel, as above, is the best way of doing it. Each bulb gets the full supply voltage. Also, each can be switched on and off independently without affecting the others.

In a house, the electricity supplier's cable branches into several parallel circuits. These carry power to the lights, cooker, and mains sockets. In the **consumer unit** ('fuse box'), each circuit passes through a fuse or circuit breaker (see next page). Plug-in appliances like irons and hairdriers also have a fuse in their plug.

## Questions

1 In a house, why are the bulbs and other mains appliances connected in parallel?

2 What would you find in a consumer unit?

## Two-way switches

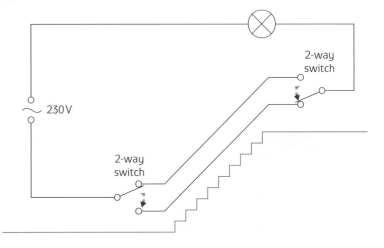

In most houses, you can turn the landing light on or off using upstairs or downstairs switches. These have two contacts instead of one. They are **two-way switches**. If both switches are up or down, then a current flows through the bulb. But if one is up and the other is down, the circuit is broken. Each switch reverses the effect of the other.

*Using a two-way switch.*

*A residual current circuit breaker (RCCB).*

## Circuit breakers

Some 'fuse boxes' have **circuit breakers** in them instead of fuses. A circuit breaker is an automatic switch which turns off the current if this gets too high. Unlike a fuse, it can be reset.

For extra safety, when using extension cables to lawnmowers and hedgetrimmers, you should use a **residual current circuit breaker (RCCB)**, as on the left. This detects whether any current is flowing to earth – perhaps through someone touching a wire that has been cut. It switches off the current before any harm can be done.

## More about a.c. and d.c.

Alternating current (a.c.) is easier to generate than one-way **direct current** (d.c.) of the type that flows from a battery.

You can see the difference between a.c. and d.c. using an **oscilloscope**. This can plot a graph very rapidly, over and over again, showing how the voltage of a supply varies with time:

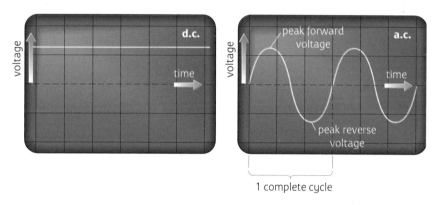

A d.c. voltage is steady, and always in the same direction. An a.c. voltage rises to a peak (maximum), falls to zero, changes direction... and so on, many times every second.

In the UK, the **mains frequency** is 50 **hertz** (Hz). This means that there are 50 complete backwards-and-forwards cycles every second.

### Did you know?

**Mains voltage**

An a.c. voltage is always changing. But mains voltage in the UK is given as 230 V. That is because the 230 V is a special type of average. It is equal to the steady d.c. voltage which would produce the same heating effect in, for example, a kettle, iron, or toaster.

## Questions

**3 a** What does a circuit breaker do?

**b** What advantage does a circuit breaker have over a fuse?

**4** Copy and complete the diagram on the right to show how the bulb can be controlled by either of the switches.

**5** What is the difference between a.c. and d.c.?

**6** In the UK, *mains frequency is 50 Hz.* Explain what this means.

# Electricity from magnetism

You don't need batteries to produce a current: just a wire, a magnet, and movement.

## Generating a voltage in a wire

If you move a wire across a magnetic field, as shown below left, a small voltage is generated in the wire. The effect is called **electromagnetic induction**. Scientifically speaking, a voltage is **induced** in the wire. As the wire is part of a complete circuit, the voltage makes a current flow.

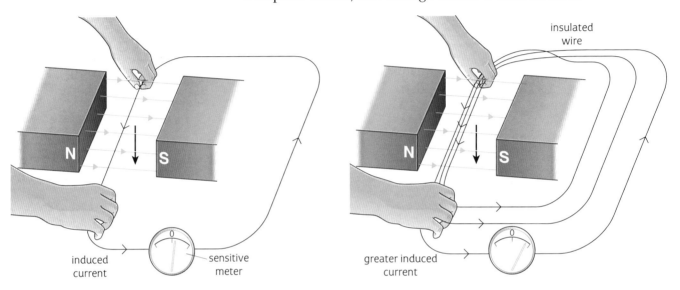

induced current — sensitive meter

greater induced current

insulated wire

To increase the induced voltage (and current), you can:

- Move the wire faster.
- Use a stronger magnet.
- Increase the length of wire in the field – for example, by looping the wire through the field several times, as shown above right.

These results are summed up by **Faraday's law**, given here in simplified form:

> Whenever a conductor cuts through magnetic field lines, a voltage is generated. The faster the field lines are cut, the greater the voltage. If no field lines are cut there is no voltage.

## Generating a voltage in a coil

At the top of the next page, you can see another way of inducing a voltage (and current) in a wire. This time, it is the magnet which is being moved rather than the wire. But the result is the same: field lines are being cut.

### Questions

1 In the experiment shown above, what would be the effect of:

   **a** moving the wire upwards rather than downwards?

   **b** holding the wire still?

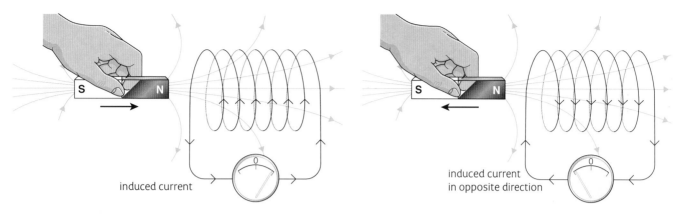

induced current

induced current
in opposite direction

To increase the induced voltage (and current), you can:

- Move the magnet faster.
- Use a stronger magnet.
- Put more turns on the coil.

If you pull the magnet *out of* the coil, as shown above right, the direction of the induced voltage (and current) is reversed. Turning the magnet round, so that the S pole goes in and out, rather than the N pole, also reverses the current direction. If you hold the magnet still, no field lines are cut, so there is no induced voltage or current.

*Guitar pick-ups are tiny coils with magnets inside them. The magnets magnetize the steel strings. When the strings vibrate, current is induced in the coils, boosted by an amplifier, and used to produce sound.*

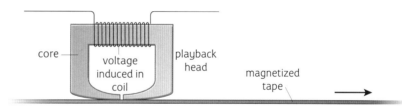

The playback heads in audio and video cassette recorders contain tiny coils. A tiny, varying voltage is induced (generated) in the coil as the magnetized tape passes over it. In this way, the magnetized patterns on the tape are changed into electrical signals. These are amplified and used to reproduce the original sound or picture.

## Questions

**2** In the experiment on the opposite page, a current is being induced in a wire. What would be the effect of:

  **a** using a stronger magnet?

  **b** moving the wire faster?

  **c** moving the wire along the magnetic field lines instead of across them?

**3** In the experiment at the top of the page, what would be the effect of:

  **a** moving the magnet faster?

  **b** turning the magnet round, so that the S pole is pushed into the coil?

  **c** putting more turns on the coil?

# Generators and transformers

**This spread should help you to**
- explain how generators work
- describe what transformers do

Most of our electricity comes from huge **generators** in power stations. There are smaller generators in cars and motorcycles. All use electromagnetic induction. Most generate **alternating current (a.c.)**. These are also known as **alternators**.

## A simple a.c. generator (alternator)

The alternator below is supplying current to a small bulb. The **coil** is rotated by turning the shaft. The **slip rings** rotate with the coil. The **brushes** are usually made of carbon. They rub against the slip rings and keep the coil connected to the outside part of the circuit.

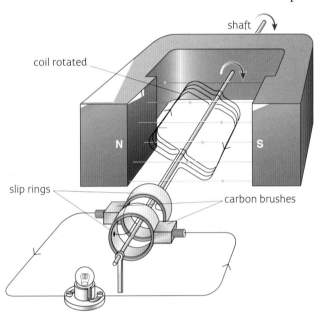

*A simple a.c. generator, connected to a bulb.*

*Graph showing the generator's a.c. output.*

When the coil is rotated, it cuts magnetic field lines, so a voltage is generated. This makes a current flow. As the coil rotates, each side travels upwards, downwards, upwards, downwards... and so on, through the field. So the current flows backwards, forwards... and so on. In other words, it is a.c.

The voltage (and current) from the generator can be increased by:

- putting more turns on the coil.
- using a bigger coil.
- using a stronger magnet.
- rotating the coil faster.

Faster rotation increases the frequency of the a.c. Mains generators must keep a steady frequency: 50 Hz (cycles per second) in the UK.

## Questions

1 What does an alternator do?
2 If the alternator above were given a stronger magnet, how would this affect its output?

*An alternator in a car.*

*This power adaptor contains a step-down transformer to reduce the 230 volts from the mains to about 9 volts. (It also contains a rectifier to change the a.c. to d.c.)*

## Practical alternators

These usually have fixed coils arranged around a rotating electromagnet. This means that the current generated does not have to flow through sliding contacts, which might overheat.

Cars need 'one-way' direct current (d.c.) for recharging the battery and running other circuits. They use a device called a **rectifier** to change the alternator's a.c. output to d.c.

## Transformers

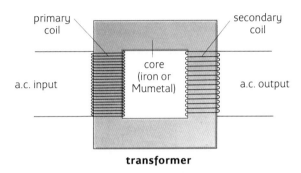

**transformer**

An a.c. voltage can be changed using a **transformer** like the one above. The **primary coil** is used as an electromagnet. When connected to an a.c. supply, it produces an alternating magnetic field. This induces a voltage in the **secondary coil** – as would happen if you could move a magnet in and out of the coil very fast.

The output voltage depends on how many turns there are on each coil. For example, if the secondary coil has *half* the turns of the primary, the output voltage is *half* the input voltage. **Step-up transformers** increase voltage, **step-down transformers** reduce it.

Transformers don't give you something for nothing. If they *increase* voltage, they *decrease* the current, and vice versa.

## Questions

3 Current can be a.c. or d.c.
  **a** What do a.c. and d.c. stand for?
  **b** Which type is generated by an alternator?
  **c** Which type is used by a transformer?
4 What job is done by:
  **a** a step-up transformer?
  **b** a step-down transformer?

5 Look at the simple alternator on the opposite page.
  **a** Why does this alternator need slip rings?
  **b** If the alternator were turned faster, how would its output change?
  **c** Most practical alternators have a different layout from the simple type shown. How are they different?
  **d** Why do some alternators have a rectifier fitted?

# KILLER cables

A 132 000 volt overhead cable can push more than enough current through someone to kill them. To prevent accidents, the cables are suspended way above roof-top height. And the pylons are built so that people can't climb them. However, accidents have occurred when kite lines have touched cables.

# DEADLY playground

Every year, over 50 children are killed or seriously injured while playing on railway lines. Electrified track is especially dangerous. Contact with the live rail doesn't always kill. But it can cause serious burns as current flows through arms or legs to the ground.

# Battery BURN

Most people don't expect a 12 volt car battery to be dangerous. But if a spanner is accidentally connected across the wires from the battery, the surge of current could be enough to burn you or start a fire. Wise mechanics disconnect the battery before starting work.

# FIRE hazards

In the home, people are more at risk from electrical fires than they are from electric shocks. Here are some of the causes:

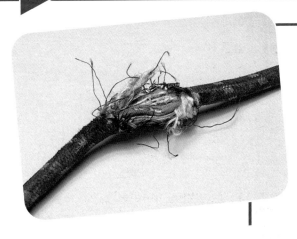

**Frayed wiring**  Broken strands of wire can mean that a cable has a high resistance at one point. So heat is given off when current flows through. It may be enough to melt the insulation and cause a fire.

**Dirty plug pins**  These give a high resistance where they connect with the socket. When a current flows through, the plug may overheat.

**Faulty appliances**  Each year, many house fires are caused by faulty washing machines and TVs. You can't tell when faults are going to develop, so the safest thing to do is not to leave appliances like this switched on when you are asleep or out of the house.

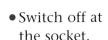

## Safety first

If an accident like this happens, you must do the following before giving any help to the person:

- Switch off at the socket.
- Pull out the plug.

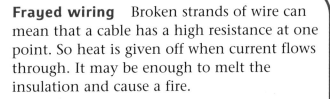

## Talking points

See if you can find out the reason for each of the following:
- Bathroom lights have to be switched on and off by a pull-cord, rather than an ordinary switch.
- Extension leads shouldn't be coiled up tightly when in use.
- Electric lawnmowers, hedgetrimmers, and drills should always be used with a 'power breaker' safety adaptor.
- A TV set shouldn't be left on stand-by overnight or when you are out.

# Lightning capital

Phoenix, Arizona, USA has been called the lightning capital of the world. If you don't like thunderstorms, stay away from Phoenix!

Lightning is caused when charge builds up on one part of a cloud and then rapidly flows – as a spark – to another cloud or the ground. But why does charge build up? A simple explanation might be that ice particles 'rub' against the air as they are sucked up through the cloud. However, the real picture is much more complicated than that.

# Lightning strikes

They say that lightning never strikes twice. But that isn't true. It can strike again . . . and again.

In the First World War, Major Summerford was wounded in Flanders, not by the enemy, but by a flash of lightning which knocked him off his horse. Six years later, he was struck by lightning again while fishing – and yet again two years later when he was out for a walk. Even after his death in 1932, he did not rest in peace. Lightning shattered his tombstone.

# Ions in the air

Ions are charged atoms or molecules. There are plenty floating around in the air. For example, every time there is a lightning flash, the discharge produces ions.

It has been claimed that some ions in the air improve your mood or your health, although there is no firm evidence for this. You can buy small electrical machines to ionize the air in your home. And if you think that they are going to make you feel better, you probably will!

# Safety cage

The worker inside the cage is quite safe, despite the 2.5 million volt sparks from the huge high-voltage generator. The electric discharges strike the metal bars, rather than pass between them, so the cage has a shielding effect. In fact, if you ignore safety advice, some of the experiments done in a school laboratory can be much more dangerous than this one.

# Attracting dust and ash

Some things in the house seem to attract dust. For example, you can usually see dust sticking to the screen of a TV. It is pulled there by the charge that builds up on the screen. In a house, the attraction effect may be a nuisance, but it does have practical uses elsewhere. Here is an example.

**Electrostatic precipitators** are fitted to the chimneys of some power stations and factories. They reduce pollution by removing tiny bits of ash from the waste gases. The diagram shows the basic layout. As the ash and waste gases pass through the chamber, the ash is given a negative charge by the wires. The charged ash is attracted to the positive plates and sticks to them. When shaken from the plates, it is collected in the tray at the bottom.

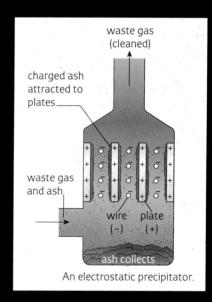

An electrostatic precipitator.

# Talking points

● The electrostatic precipitator shown above makes use of the attraction between opposite charges. By looking at earlier spreads in this chapter, see if you can find some more practical uses of the forces between charges.

● When you see a flash of lightning, the 'crash' is heard a little later. By looking up information about light and sound in the index, see if you can find out why this is. With the information you have found, could you estimate how far away lightning was if the 'crash' was heard 2 seconds after the flash?

# Power for motion

## Engines or motors?

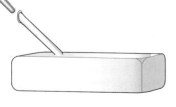

The car above is good for special occasions, but not for parking in tight spaces or getting round corners. And it is certainly not good for the environment. The exhaust gases from its huge petrol engine pollute the atmosphere.

The car on the left is more cramped and not so good for long distances. But it is less polluting. It is powered by an electric motor, so it doesn't have an exhaust pipe. If everyone drove cars like this, conditions in city centres would be much more pleasant.

Electric motors are a clean and efficient way of turning the wheels. But present-day electric cars have one major problem. They need batteries. These are a relatively poor way of storing energy and must be recharged. Battery-powered cars will never have the performance or range of petrol or diesel models.

These can deliver the same amount of energy

**1 full tank of petrol**
mass: 50 kg
time to refill: 3 minutes

**150 fully charged car batteries**
mass: 1500 kg (1.5 tonnes)
time to recharge: 3 hours

# Fuel cell future

Fortunately, there is a solution to the battery problem. It is a source of electricity called a **fuel cell**. When you feed a fuel cell with hydrogen (plus oxygen from the air), chemical reactions deliver a continuous supply of electricity. The cell doesn't need recharging. As long as you feed in the gases, the cell delivers the current, and the only waste product is water. Fuel cells have been around for years. However, the technology has only recently become cheap enough for cars.

In cars, the main problem with fuel cells is how to store the hydrogen. It isn't safe or practical to carry large cylinders of this highly inflammable gas. That is why the fuel in the tank is likely to be liquid methanol. A unit called a **reformer** produces hydrogen from the methanol using steam and catalysts.

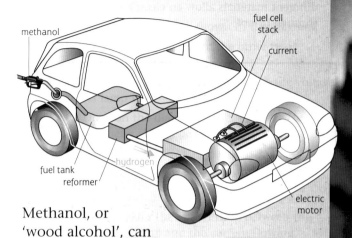

Methanol, or 'wood alcohol', can be made using plant materials grown as a renewable resource. It can also be produced from natural gas. Vehicles with fuel cells will have the range and performance of today's fuel burners but be more efficient and less polluting. The days of petrol and diesel engines may soon be over.

## An old problem

Pollution isn't a new problem. In the 1800s, horse-drawn traffic was increasing so much that it was estimated that, by the end of the century, Londoners would be up to their knees in horse manure.

## Talking points

Present-day electric cars have batteries which are recharged by plugging them in to a mains-powered charger. Their electric motors produce no pollution. Can you suggest reasons why, if everyone drove cars like this, the system would still cause atmospheric pollution?

Can you suggest reasons why cars with fuel cells in are likely to be more successful and popular than battery-powered cars?

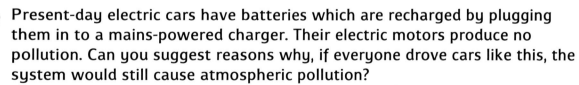

# Forces

# Module 11

A bungee jumper leaps more than 180 metres from the centre of a bridge over a river gorge. With nothing to oppose her fall, she would hit the water after 6 seconds, at a speed of 60 metres per second (135 m.p.h.). However, her fall is slowed by the resistance of the air rushing past her, and eventually stopped by the pull of the bungee rope.

# 11.01 Speed, velocity, and acceleration

## Objectives

**This spread should help you to**

- explain the difference between speed and velocity
- explain what acceleration means

## Speed

Here is a simple method of measuring speed. You could use it to work out the speed of a cyclist like the one below:

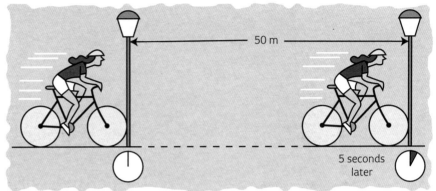

Measure the distance between two points on a road, say two lamp posts, as above. Measure the time taken to travel between these points. Then use this equation:

$$\text{speed} = \frac{\text{distance travelled}}{\text{time taken}}$$

distance in metres (m)
time in seconds (s)
speed in metres per second (m/s)

If the cyclist travels 50 m in 5 s her speed is 50/5, which is 10 m/s.

This calculation really gives her average speed, as her actual speed may vary during the 5 s. To find an actual speed, you need to know the distance travelled in the shortest time you can measure.

## Velocity

**Velocity** means speed in a particular direction. To show the direction, you can use an arrow. Or, in simple cases, you can use a + or − to show whether the motion is to the right or to the left. There are some examples below. (A velocity of +10 m/s may be written without the +, just as 10 m/s.)

*A world-class 100 metre sprinter has an average speed of about 10 m/s (or 22 miles per hour (m.p.h.)).*

## Questions

1 If a cyclist travels 40 metres in 8 seconds, what is her average speed?

2 What is the difference between *speed* and *velocity*?

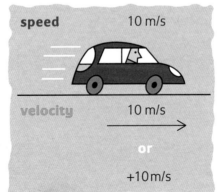

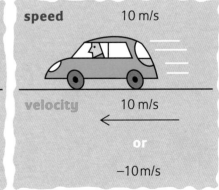

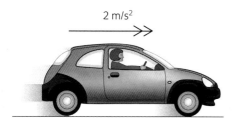

2 m/s²

| time in s | velocity in m/s |
|-----------|-----------------|
| 0 | 0 |
| 1 | 2 |
| 2 | 4 |
| 3 | 6 |
| 4 | 8 |

*The velocity of this car is increasing by 2 m/s every second. The acceleration is 2 m/s².*

## Acceleration

Something is **accelerating** if its velocity is *changing*. The velocity of the car on the left is increasing by 2 m/s every second. The car has an acceleration of 2 metres per second per second, written 2 m/s². Acceleration is calculated like this:

$$acceleration = \frac{change\ in\ velocity}{time\ taken}$$

velocity in m/s
time in s
acceleration in m/s²

In simple cases, where something is always travelling in the same direction, 'change in velocity' means the same thing as 'gain in speed'. For example, the car above left has a change in velocity of 8 m/s in 4 s. In other words, its speed goes up by 8 m/s in 4 s. So: acceleration = 8/4 = 2 m/s².

## Retardation

**Retardation** means 'deceleration'. If a car has a retardation of 2 m/s², its velocity is getting *less* by 2 m/s every second.

A retardation of 2 m/s² means the same as an acceleration of −2 m/s². Either way, the velocity is reducing by 2 m/s every second.

*The Space Shuttle uses a parachute, as well as its brakes, to produce the retardation it needs when it lands.*

## Questions

**3** A car has an acceleration of 4 m/s². Explain what this means.

Questions 4–10 are about the table below, which shows how the speed of a car changed with time.

**4** What was the car's maximum speed?

**5** For how many seconds was the car accelerating?

**6** When was the car's acceleration zero ?

**7** What was the change in speed in the first 3 seconds?

**8** What was the acceleration over the first 3 seconds?

**9** How many seconds after the start of its journey did the car start to brake?

**10** What was the retardation over the last 4 seconds?

| Time in seconds | 0 | 1 | 2 | 3 | 4 | 5 | 6 | 7 | 8 | 9 | 10 | 11 | 12 | 13 | 14 | 15 |
|-----------------|---|---|---|---|----|----|----|----|----|----|----|----|----|----|----|----|
| Speed in m/s | 0 | 3 | 6 | 9 | 12 | 12 | 12 | 12 | 12 | 12 | 10 | 8 | 6 | 4 | 2 | 0 |

*A 'black box' flight recorder isn't black at all!*

Large passenger aircraft carry 'black box' flight recorders like the one on the left. One job of a recorder is to record – on magnetic wire – the position of the aircraft throughout the flight. In the very unlikely event of a crash, the box is tough enough to survive. Engineers can use data from it to work out how fast the aircraft was travelling before the accident, how the speed and direction were changing, and whether this was normal.

### Trolley experiments

Below, you can see a simpler method of recording motion, using paper tape. The 'vehicle' being studied is a trolley moving on a laboratory bench. As the trolley is pulled across the bench, it trails a paper tape behind it. The tape passes through a timer. This marks dots on the tape at regular intervals of time (every 1/50 second).

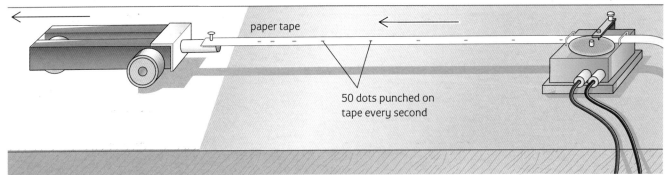

trolley pulled across bench

ticker-tape timer

paper tape

50 dots punched on tape every second

On the next page are the results of five different 'runs' with the trolley. For each one, you can work out the motion of the trolley by seeing how the distance between the dots changes. The faster the trolley, the further it travelled in each 1/50 second, so the bigger the distance between the dots.

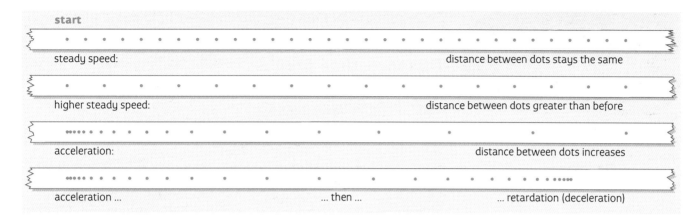

**start**

steady speed:            distance between dots stays the same

higher steady speed:          distance between dots greater than before

acceleration:            distance between dots increases

acceleration ...         ... then ...         ... retardation (deceleration)

## More trolley experiments

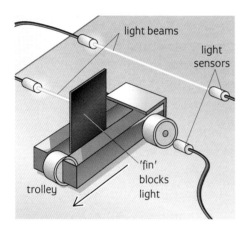

The motion of a trolley can also be studied using light sensors linked to a datalogger. The datalogger is connected to a computer so that its results can be displayed as a graph.

The trolley on the left has a 'fin' on the top. As the fin moves past each sensor, the module measures the time for which the light beam is blocked: the faster the trolley, the shorter the time. The computer can use this information to work out the speed of the trolley. Using measurements taken at different positions along the bench, it can show how the speed of the trolley changed.

# Questions

**1** Tapes A–D below are from trolley experiments. Which one shows each of the following?

  **a** Acceleration, then a steady speed.

  **b** A steady speed, then retardation (deceleration) until stopped.

  **c** A steady speed, then acceleration, then a higher steady speed.

**2** A trolley travelling at a steady speed loses speed, stops, then accelerates. Copy the blank tape below. Mark in the pattern of dots you might expect to see.

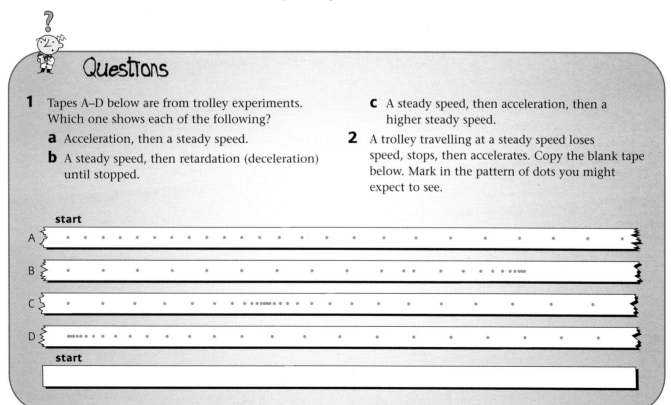

## 11.03 Motion graphs

**Objectives**

**This spread should help you to**
- interpret distance–time graphs and speed–time graphs

From motion graphs, you can work out how fast something is moving, and whether it is accelerating.

## Distance–time graphs

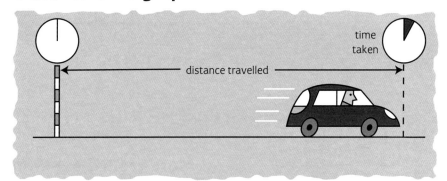

The car above is travelling along a straight road. Every second (s), its distance from the post is measured, in metres (m). Here are four examples of the graphs you might get from the readings:

**A** *Car travelling at a **steady speed***

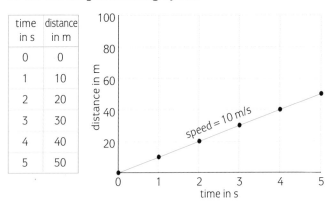

| time in s | distance in m |
|---|---|
| 0 | 0 |
| 1 | 10 |
| 2 | 20 |
| 3 | 30 |
| 4 | 40 |
| 5 | 50 |

*The line rises 10m on the distance scale for every 1s on the time scale. So the speed is 10m/s.*

**B** *Car travelling at a **higher steady speed***

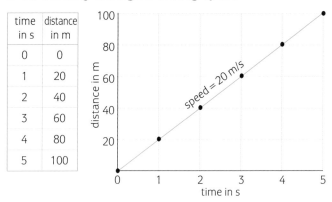

| time in s | distance in m |
|---|---|
| 0 | 0 |
| 1 | 20 |
| 2 | 40 |
| 3 | 60 |
| 4 | 80 |
| 5 | 100 |

*The line is steeper. It rises 20m on the distance scale for every 1s on the time scale. So the speed is 20m/s.*

**C** *Car **accelerating***

| time in s | distance in m |
|---|---|
| 0 | 0 |
| 1 | 10 |
| 2 | 25 |
| 3 | 45 |
| 4 | 70 |
| 5 | 100 |

*The speed rises. So the car travels further each second than the one before, and the line curves upwards.*

**D** *Car **stationary** (stopped)*

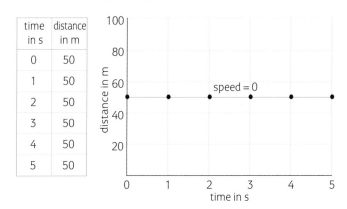

| time in s | distance in m |
|---|---|
| 0 | 50 |
| 1 | 50 |
| 2 | 50 |
| 3 | 50 |
| 4 | 50 |
| 5 | 50 |

*The car is parked 50m from the post, so this distance stays the same.*

## Speed–time graphs

Below are two examples of the graphs you might get if you measure the speed of a car every second as it travels along a straight road.

Don't confuse these graphs with distance–time graphs! The shapes may look the same, but their meaning is very different.

**E** *Car travelling at a **steady speed***

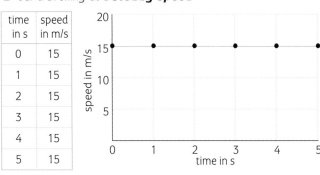

| time in s | speed in m/s |
|---|---|
| 0 | 15 |
| 1 | 15 |
| 2 | 15 |
| 3 | 15 |
| 4 | 15 |
| 5 | 15 |

*The speed stays the same, so the line stays at the same level.*

**F** *Car **accelerating***

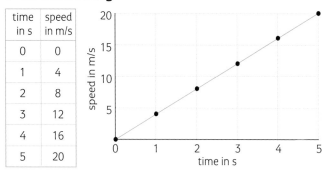

| time in s | speed in m/s |
|---|---|
| 0 | 0 |
| 1 | 4 |
| 2 | 8 |
| 3 | 12 |
| 4 | 16 |
| 5 | 20 |

*As the car gains speed, the line rises 4 m/s on the speed scale for every 1 s on the time scale.*

**Velocity–time graphs** The graphs above could have their vertical axis labelled 'velocity in m/s' rather than 'speed in m/s'. In simple cases, where something is always travelling in the same direction, a speed–time graph and a velocity–time graph look exactly the same.

## Questions

*To answer these questions, you will need the equations for speed and for acceleration in the previous spread. So write these down before you start.*

**1**

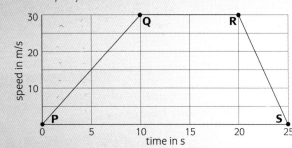

The speed–time graph above is for a motor cycle travelling along a straight road.

**a** What is the motor cycle doing betweens points

   **i** P and Q?   **ii** Q and R?   **iii** R and S?

**b** What is the motor cycle's maximum speed?

**c** For how many seconds is the motor cycle moving?

**d** How much speed does it gain in the first 10 seconds?

**e** What is the acceleration in the first 10 seconds?

**2**

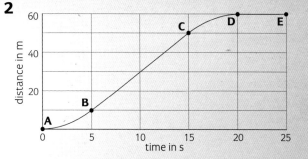

The distance–time graph above is for another motor cycle travelling along a straight road.

**a** What is the motor cycle doing between points **D** and **E** on the graph?

**b** What is the speed of the motor cycle between **B** and **C**?

# Forces and gravity

**This spread should help you to**

- give examples of forces and how they are measured
- explain what weight and gravitational field strength are

**Did you know?**

**Typical forces**

| | |
|---|---|
| Force to switch on a bathroom light... | 10 N |
| Force to pull open a drinks can... | 20 N |
| Force to lift a heavy suitcase... | 200 N |
| Force from a jet engine... | 250 000 N |

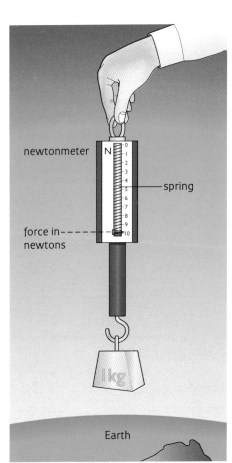

newtonmeter

spring

force in newtons

1 kg

Earth

A **force** is a push or pull. It is measured in **newtons** (N). You can see some typical force values in the table below left.

Small forces can be measured using a spring balance (called a **newtonmeter**) like the one at the bottom of the page. The greater the force, the more the spring is stretched, and the higher the reading on the scale.

Here are some examples of forces:

**Tension** *The force in a stretched material.*

**Weight** *The downward pull of gravity.*

**Friction** *The force that tries to stop one thing sliding past another.*

**Air resistance** *Another type of friction.*

## Gravitational force

If you hang something from the end of a spring balance, as on the left, you can measure a downward pull from the Earth. The pull is called a **gravitational force**.

No one knows what causes gravitational force. But several things are known about it:

- All masses attract each other. The greater the masses, the stronger the force.
- The closer the masses, the stronger the force.

The force between everyday objects is far too weak to measure. It only becomes strong if one of the objects has a huge mass, like the Earth.

## Weight and gravitational field strength

**Weight** is another name for the gravitational force from the Earth. It is measured in N, just like other forces.

*The more mass something has, the more it weighs.*

On Earth, each kilogram (kg) of matter weighs 10N. The Earth has a **gravitational field strength** of 10 newtons per kilogram (N/kg). This is called *g*.

If you know the mass of something, you can work out its weight like this:

weight = mass × *g*
in N        in kg

where *g* is 10N/kg on Earth.

For example, the person in the diagram above has a mass of 50 kg.

So:
  weight =   50   ×   10   =   500 N

People often use the word 'weight' when they really mean 'mass'. The person above doesn't 'weigh' 50 kg. He has a *mass* of 50 kg and a *weight* of 500 N.

## Questions

**1**  *kg   N*
What do each of the above stand for?

**2**  Which of the above would you use to measure:

  **a**  mass?

  **b**  force?

  **c**  weight?

## Questions

**3**  In the diagram on the right, a climber is swinging on a rope, and moving fast.

Draw a simple version of the diagram.

Show *three* forces acting on the climber.

Name the three forces by labelling them.

**4**  Work out the weights of each of the masses below, assuming that *g* is 10N/kg.

### Objectives

**This spread should help you to**

- describe how friction can be useful or a nuisance
- give examples of friction from air and water

Friction is the force that tries to stop materials sliding past each other. There is friction between your hands when you rub them together, and friction between your shoes and the ground when you walk along. Air resistance is another type of friction. It slows you down when you ride a bike.

Friction can be useful or it can be a nuisance. Here are some examples, on a bike:

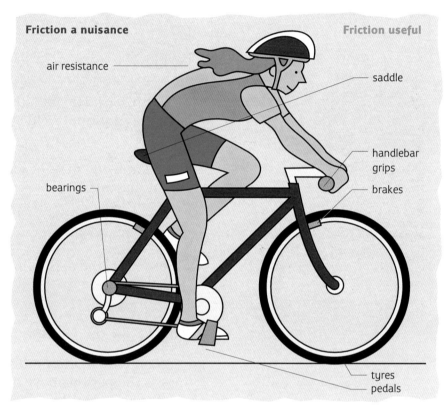

Friction a nuisance ... Friction useful

air resistance
saddle
handlebar grips
bearings
brakes
tyres
pedals

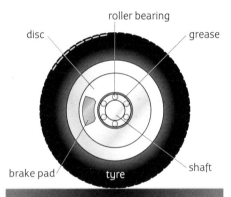

roller bearing
disc
grease
shaft
brake pad
tyre

*Parts of a car wheel (see question 3).*

### Using friction

Without friction between the tyres and the ground, you would not be able to ride a bike. It would be like riding on ice. You could not speed up, turn, or stop.

Brakes rely on friction. The wheels of a cycle are slowed by pressing rubber blocks against the rims. The wheels of a car are slowed by pressing fibre pads against metal discs attached to the wheels. But none of these brakes would be any good without friction between the tyres and the ground.

### Problems with friction

Friction slows moving things and produces heat. In machinery, grease and oil are used to reduce friction so that moving parts do not overheat and seize up. Ball bearings and roller bearings also reduce friction. Their rolling action means that a wheel does not rub against its shaft.

### Questions

1. Give one place on a bike where friction is a nuisance.

2. Give one place on a bike where friction is needed. Say *why* the friction is needed there.

## Friction from air and water

Air and water 'rub' against things when they they flow past them. For example, when a car is travelling fast, air resistance is by far the largest frictional force pulling against it.

If a car could speed along without air resistance, it would use much less fuel. Car designers cannot get rid of air resistance, but they can give the car a streamlined shape to reduce it as much as possible.

Air resistance increases with speed. So drivers can reduce air resistance and save fuel by not driving so fast.

*Reducing friction from air. Car bodies are specially shaped to smooth the airflow past them and reduce air resistance. A low 'front-on' area also helps.*

*Reducing friction from water. When this hydrofoil is going fast, it rises up on 'water skis' to reduce the friction between its hull and the water.*

## Questions

**3** Look at the diagram on the opposite page, showing the parts of a car wheel.

   **a** Give *two* places on the wheel where friction is useful.

   **b** Give *one* place where friction is a nuisance.

   **c** What features does the wheel have to reduce friction at the place you chose in part **b**?

   **d** Give *two* reasons why it is important to reduce the friction at the place you chose in part **b**.

**4** Look at the photograph on the right. List the features you can see for reducing friction.

**5** Cars are slowed down by the force of air resistance.

   **a** Describe *two* ways in which the force of air resistance on a car can be reduced.

   **b** What are the advantages of reducing air resistance on a car?

# Balanced forces

No one is winning the tug-of-war match above, and the knot in the middle doesn't move. The two forces on it are balanced. They cancel each other out. Their combined effect is zero.

This spread is about how things behave when there are no forces acting, or the forces are balanced.

## Balanced forces when still

*When the girl is stationary, the forces on her are balanced.*

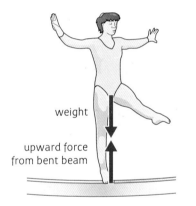

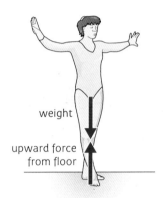

weight

upward force from bent beam

weight

upward force from floor

When the girl stands on the beam, it bends, until the springiness of the wood produces enough upward force to support her weight. Then, the forces on the girl are balanced, and she is stationary (still). The floor isn't as springy as the beam, but it too produces an upward force to equal the girl's weight when she stands on it.

## Newton's first law of motion

On Earth, unpowered vehicles quickly come to rest – slowed by the force of friction. But how would they behave if there were *no* forces acting? According to Sir Isaac Newton's **first law of motion**:

If something has no force on it, it will...

...if still, stay still;
...if moving, keep moving at a steady velocity (steady speed in a straight line).

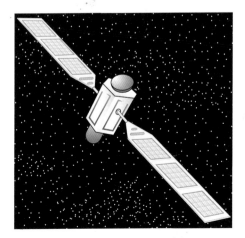

*Deep in space, with no frictional forces to slow it down, an unpowered spacecraft will keep moving for ever.*

## Balanced forces when moving

If something is moving, and the forces on it are balanced, it behaves as if there is no force acting. It keeps moving at a steady speed in a straight line, as predicted by Newton's first law. Here are two examples of moving things with balanced forces on them:

A skydiver with steady velocity (steady speed in a straight line).

A skater with steady velocity (steady speed in a straight line).

## Terminal speed

A skydiver jumps from a helicopter. As her speed rises, the air resistance on her increases until it matches her weight. Then, the two forces are balanced, and she reaches a steady speed. This is called her **terminal speed** (or **terminal velocity**). It is usually about 60 m/s (120 m.p.h.), though the actual value depends on air conditions, as well as the size, shape, and weight of the skydiver.

When a skydiver is falling at her terminal speed, the forces on her are balanced.

When the skydiver opens her parachute, the extra area of material increases the air resistance. So she loses speed rapidly until the forces are again in balance at a new, slower, terminal speed.

## Questions

1. If the forces on something are balanced, which of the following could it be doing? (There may be more than one answer.)

   **a** speeding up   **b** slowing down

   **c** staying still   **d** moving at a steady speed in a straight line

2. The parachutist on the right is descending at a steady speed.

   **a** What name is given to this speed?

   **b** Copy the diagram. Mark in and label another force acting.

   **c** How does this force compare with the weight?

   **d** If the parachutist used a larger parachute, how would this affect the steady speed reached? Explain why.

weight

# Unbalanced forces

## Objectives

**This spread should help you to**

- describe how things behave if the forces on them are unbalanced

On Earth, most things have more than one force on them. For example, a falling stone has weight and air resistance. This spread is about how things behave when the forces on them are unbalanced.

## Resultant force

If the forces on something are unbalanced, they have a combined effect called the **resultant** force. The chart below gives some examples of the resultant of two forces. (N = newton.)

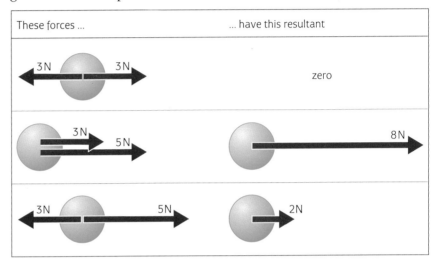

## Mass and motion

All things resist a change in speed – even if their speed is zero. If an object is at rest, it takes a force to make it move. If it is moving, it takes a force to make it go faster or slower.

The more mass something has, the more it resists any change in motion. In other words, the more difficult it is to accelerate.

## Questions

1  A stone has two forces on it: 10 N downwards and 4 N upwards.

   **a** Draw a diagram to show the forces on the stone.

   **b** What is the resultant force?

   **c** What is the direction of this force?

*This tanker has so much mass that, once it is moving, it is extremely difficult to stop.*

## The effect of a resultant force

Imagine a truck on a road...

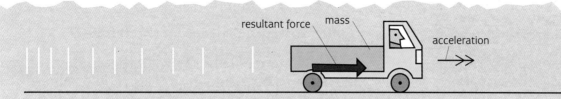

If there is a resultant force on the truck, it will accelerate – in the same direction as this force.

Increasing the resultant force produces more acceleration.

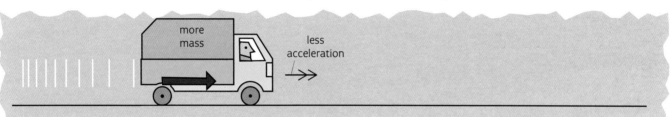

But if the mass of the truck is increased, you get less acceleration for the same force.

## Questions

**2** Diagram **A** on the right shows two forces on a car.

   **a** What is the direction of the resultant force?

   **b** Would you expect the car to *gain speed* or *lose speed*?

   **c** If the car had more mass, what effect would this have?

   **d** If the resultant force on the car were greater, what effect would this have?

**3** Diagram **B** on the right shows two forces on another car.

   **a** What is the direction of the resultant force?

   **b** Would you expect this car to *gain speed* or *lose speed*? Give a reason for your answer.

**c** What would the car do if the two forces were equal?

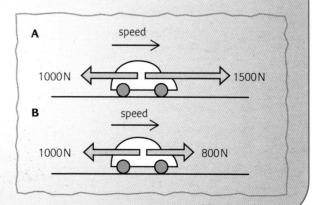

**11.08**

# Speed and safety

## Objectives

**This spread should help you to**

- describe the factors which affect a car's stopping distance
- describe features which can make a car safer for its passengers

## Stopping distance

In an emergency, the driver of a car may have to react quickly and apply the brakes to stop the car.

A car's **stopping distance** depends on two things:

- The **thinking distance**. This is how far the car travels *before* the brakes are applied, while the driver is still reacting.
- The **braking distance**. This is how far the car then travels, *after* the brakes have been applied.

It takes an average driver more than half a second to react and press the brake pedal. This is the driver's **reaction time**. During this time, the car does not slow down. For example:

If a car has a speed of 20 m/s (metres per second), and the driver has a reaction time of 0.5 s, the car will travel 10 m in that time. At a higher speed, the thinking distance would be greater.

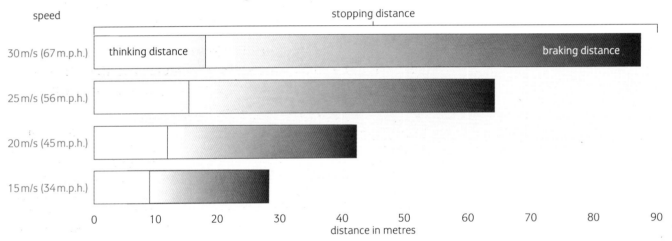

The chart above shows the stopping distances for a car at different speeds. They are average figures for a dry road. The actual stopping distance may be *greater*. Here are some of the reasons why:

The *driver* may have a slower reaction time, because of...

- tiredness
- poor weather conditions affecting visibility
- the effects of alcohol or drugs

The *brakes* may take longer to stop the car, because of...

- a wet or icy road
- a heavy load in the car
- worn brakes or tyres

## Questions

1. For a car, what is meant by each of these?

   **a** thinking distance

   **b** braking distance

   **c** stopping distance

2. Give *two* reasons why the thinking distance may be greater than normal.

130

*If there isn't enough friction between its tyres and the road, a car will skid.*

## Braking, friction, and skidding

To stop quickly, a car must lose speed rapidly. A high braking force is needed for this. It is provided by the friction between the tyres and the road. But there is a limit to the amount of friction ('grip') that the tyres can supply. If the brakes are put on too strongly, the wheels will 'lock up' (stop turning) and the car will skid.

## Safety features

In a collision, a car stops, but its passengers keep moving... until something stops them as well. The 'something' could be the steering wheel or windscreen, and the impact could cause injury or death. That is why modern cars have these safety features:

**Seat belts**  These stop the passengers hitting the windscreen or other hard parts of the car's inside.

**Air bags**  These inflate in a collision. They cushion the passengers from the effects of any impact.

**Crumple zone**  The front section of a car is a 'crumple zone'. It is designed to collapse steadily in a crash so that the seat belts and air bags can slow the passengers less violently.

*This test shows how a car's front 'crumple zone' collapses in a collision so that the impact is less violent for the passengers. (The passenger compartment forms a rigid cage which is designed not to collapse.)*

## Questions

**3** Describe *three* features that a modern car has to make the effects of a collision less harmful to the passengers.

**4** Cutting your speed is the best safety feature of all. Which of the following are reduced if a car travels more slowly? (You can choose more than one answer.)

  **a** Driver's reaction time

  **b** Thinking distance

  **c** Braking distance

  **d** Risk of serious injury

**5** In the chart on the opposite page, what is the thinking distance: **a** at 25 m/s?  **b** at 30 m/s?

**6** Alcohol slows people's reactions. If a driver has a reaction time of 2 s, what will his thinking distance be at 25 m/s (56 m.p.h)?
(You may need an equation from the box below to answer this.)

$$\text{speed} = \frac{\text{distance}}{\text{time}} \qquad \text{So: distance} = \text{speed} \times \text{time}$$

distance in metres (m); time in seconds (s); speed in m/s.

Forces are always pushes or pulls between *two* things. So they always occur in pairs. One force acts on one thing. Its equal but opposite partner acts on the other. The paired forces are known as the **action** and the **reaction**. But it doesn't matter which you call which. One cannot exist without the other.

Here are some examples of action–reaction pairs:

Earth pulls downwards on skydiver

skydiver pulls upwards on Earth

runner pushes backwards on ground

ground pushes forwards on runner

forward force on bullet: bullet shoots out

backward force on gun: gun recoils

## Newton's third law of motion

Sir Isaac Newton was the first to realise that forces occur in pairs. Here is his **third law of motion**, in two versions:

> For every action there is an equal and opposite reaction.
>
> or
>
> If A pushes on B, then B pushes on A with an equal but opposite force.

*If forces always occur in pairs, why don't they cancel each other out?*

**ANSWER**
The two forces act on different things, not the same thing.

*If falling things are pulled downwards by gravity, why isn't the Earth pulled upwards?*

**ANSWER**
It is! But the Earth is so massive that the upward force on it has too small an effect to be noticed.

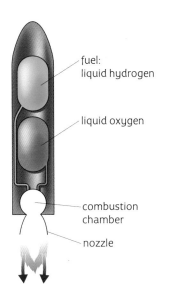

fuel: liquid hydrogen

liquid oxygen

combustion chamber

nozzle

*A rocket. As hot gas is pushed downwards, the rocket is pushed upwards.*

## Rockets and jets

Rockets and jets use the action–reaction idea. They push out a huge mass of gas in one direction so that they get pushed in the opposite direction.

**Rocket engines** have a combustion chamber where fuel is mixed with oxygen, and burnt. This produces lots of hot gas, which expands and rushes out of the nozzle.

In a rocket, the fuel and oxygen are stored either as cold liquids, or in chemicals which have been compressed into solid pellets.

**Jet engines** also push out lots of gas. But the gas is mainly air, drawn in by a huge fan.

Most of the air is pushed out by the fan. But some goes into the part of the engine that drives the fan. This is how it is used. The air is compressed, then mixed with fuel in a combustion chamber, so that the fuel burns violently. This produces lots of hot gas, which expands and rushes out of the engine. As it does so, it pushes a turbine round. The spinning turbine drives the compressor and the fan.

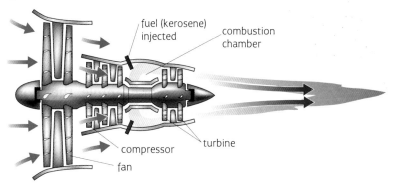

fuel (kerosene) injected

combustion chamber

turbine

compressor

fan

*A jet engine. As air and hot gas are pushed backwards, the engine is pushed forwards.*

## Questions

1 The person on the right weighs 500 N (newtons). The diagram shows the force of his feet pressing on the ground.

   **a** Copy the diagram. Label the size of the force (in N).

   **b** The ground pushes on the person's feet. Draw in this force and label its size (in N).

2 When a gun is fired, it pushes the bullet forwards. Why does the gun recoil backwards?

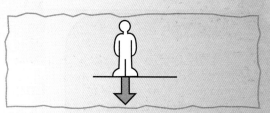

3 In the diagram on the opposite page, the forces on a runner and on the ground are equal. The runner moves forwards, but the ground doesn't seem to move backwards. Why not?

# Kinetic energy

This skater has energy of motion, **or kinetic energy**. With more mass or a higher speed, he would have more kinetic energy.

The kinetic energy (KE) of a moving object can be calculated like this:

$$KE = \tfrac{1}{2}mv^2$$

*m* is the mass of the object in kg

*v* is the speed of the object in metres per second (m/s)

Here are two examples:

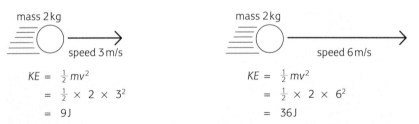

mass 2 kg     speed 3 m/s

$$KE = \tfrac{1}{2}mv^2$$
$$= \tfrac{1}{2} \times 2 \times 3^2$$
$$= 9\,J$$

mass 2 kg     speed 6 m/s

$$KE = \tfrac{1}{2}mv^2$$
$$= \tfrac{1}{2} \times 2 \times 6^2$$
$$= 36\,J$$

## Speed dangers

The above calculations show that if the speed of something *doubles*, its has *four times* as much kinetic energy. This is one of the reasons why road safety experts say that 'speed kills'. Think of the effect on a car which doubles its speed. If the car brakes normally, it will need about four times the distance to stop. If, instead, it hits a crash barrier, or another car, or a pedestrian, it will cause much more damage or injury because of all the extra energy it has to lose.

*Extra speed means much more kinetic energy, which can be dangerous.*

## Losing kinetic energy

Things lose kinetic energy when they slow down. In most cases, friction is the force that slows them, and the kinetic energy is changed into heat (thermal energy). Here are two examples:

When a Space Shuttle re-enters the atmosphere, it is slowed by friction from the air. The Shuttle is covered with heat-resistant tiles (seen here blackened by the heat after a flight) to stop it burning up as its kinetic energy is changed into heat.

When its brakes are applied, a car loses speed. The brakes use a rubbing effect, friction, to slow down the wheels. As the car's kinetic energy is changed into heat, the brakes can get very hot.

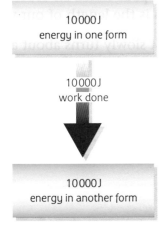

10 000 J
energy in one form

10 000 J
work done

10 000 J
energy in another form

## Work done and energy transformed

Scientifically speaking, when energy changes from one form to another, energy is **transformed**. Whenever energy is transformed, work is done. For example:

If a car loses 10 000 joules of kinetic energy because of friction, then the car does 10 000 joules of work against friction, and 10 000 joules of heat are produced. In this and every other example:

work done = energy transformed

Sometimes, scientists talk about energy being **transferred** rather than transformed, but this means the same thing.

## Questions

1 A jet engine does 5 000 000 J of work in accelerating an aircraft along a runway. How much kinetic energy would you expect the aircraft to gain, assuming that no energy is lost because of friction?

2 If the brakes of a car are applied, the car loses kinetic energy. What happens to this energy?

3 How do you calculate kinetic energy?

4 If a 4 kg brick is falling at a speed of 2 m/s:
   **a** what is the KE of the brick?
   **b** what will its KE be if it falls at twice the speed?

5 A driver thinks that if he doubles his speed, and then has to brake, the distance needed to stop his car will only be about twice what it was before. Is he correct? If not, why not?

# 11.15 Satellites in orbit

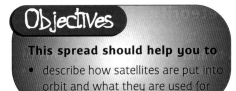

*For a low polar orbit, a speed of 29 100 km/hour (18 100 m.p.h.) is required.*

There are hundreds of satellites in orbit around the Earth. You can see some of the jobs they do on the opposite page.

To keep moving without power, satellites must be above the Earth's atmosphere, where there is no air resistance to slow them. A high orbit needs less speed than a low one. However, the launch rocket must leave the Earth faster in order to 'coast' further into space when its engines have burnt all their fuel and shut down.

Satellites that survey the Earth are often put into a low **polar orbit** – one that passes over the North and South Poles. As the Earth turns beneath them, they can scan the whole of its surface.

Communications satellites are normally put into a **geostationary orbit**. They orbit at the same rate as the Earth turns, so appear to stay in the same position in the sky. On the ground, the dish aerials sending and receiving the signals can point in a fixed direction.

## Why a satellite stays up

In the 'thought experiment' below right, an astronaut is on a tall tower, above the atmosphere. She is so strong that she can throw a ball at the speed of a rocket!

Ball A is dropped. Gravity pulls it straight downwards.

Ball B is thrown horizontally. Gravity pulls it downwards, but it also moves sideways at a steady speed.

Ball C is also thrown horizontally, but so fast that the curve of its fall matches the curve of the Earth. The ball is in orbit. And with no air resistance to slow it, it will keep its speed and stay in orbit.

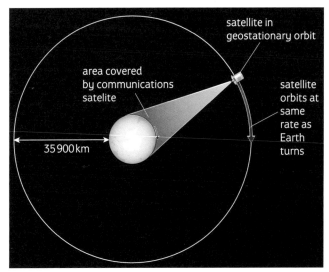

*For a geostationary orbit, a satellite must be 35 900 km above the equator, with a speed of 11 100 km/hour.*

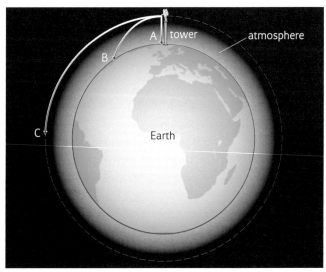

*In this 'thought experiment', ball C is thrown so fast that it never reaches the ground. (See the section above.)*

**Communications satellites** pass on telephone and TV signals from one place to another.

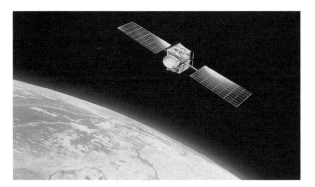

*Some TVs get their pictures from a satellite like this.*

**Monitoring satellites** study the weather and other conditions down on the Earth.

*A picture taken from a weather satellite over Europe.*

**Research satellites** Some of these carry telescopes for looking at stars and planets. Above the atmosphere, they get a much clearer view.

*This is the **Hubble Space Telescope**. It uses radio signals to send its pictures back to Earth.*

**Navigation satellites** send out radio signals which ships, aircraft, or people on the ground can use to find their position.

*This **GPS (global positioning system)** receiver uses time signals from satellites to calculate its position.*

## Questions

**1** A survey satellite is in a low polar orbit.
  **a** What is the advantage of this type of orbit?
  **b** Why must the satellite be above the atmosphere?
  **c** Give *three* other uses of satellites.

**2** A satellite is launched from a rocket when the rocket is travelling horizontally. What will happen to the satellite if the rocket is:
  **a** too fast?      **b** too slow?

**3** TV satellites are in orbit and moving. Yet, down on the ground, the dish aerials that receive the signals point in a fixed direction. How is this possible?

**4** Satellite A is put into one orbit around the Earth. Satellite B is put into a higher orbit.
  **a** Which satellite has the greater speed?
  **b** Which takes the longer time to orbit the Earth?

# Sun, stars, and galaxies

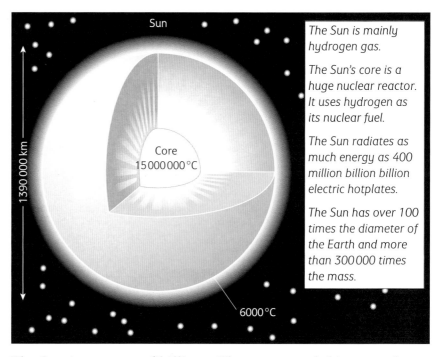

Sun

Core
15 000 000 °C

1390 000 km

6000 °C

*The Sun is mainly hydrogen gas.*

*The Sun's core is a huge nuclear reactor. It uses hydrogen as its nuclear fuel.*

*The Sun radiates as much energy as 400 million billion billion electric hotplates.*

*The Sun has over 100 times the diameter of the Earth and more than 300 000 times the mass.*

The Sun is one star of billions. There are much bigger and brighter stars. However, from Earth, all the other stars look like tiny dots because they are so much further away.

## Constellations

The brightest stars seem to form patterns in the sky. The different groups are called **constellations**. They have names like Orion, the Great Bear, and Pisces. But the stars in each constellation aren't really grouped together. For example, one star may be much further away than another, but look just as bright because it is bigger or hotter.

For practical reasons, astronomers still divide up the sky into constellations. It helps them find where different stars are.

## Light years

Light is the fastest thing there is. But it can still take a long time to cover the vast distances in space:

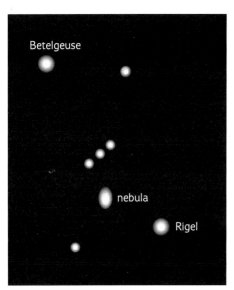

Betelgeuse

nebula

Rigel

*The constellation of Orion. Its stars aren't really in a group. Rigel is nearly twice as far away as Betelgeuse.*

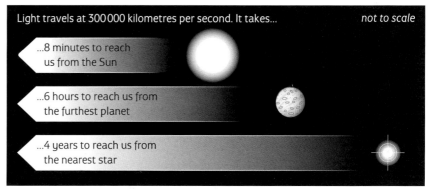

Light travels at 300 000 kilometres per second. It takes...     *not to scale*

...8 minutes to reach us from the Sun

...6 hours to reach us from the furthest planet

...4 years to reach us from the nearest star

Astronomers have special units for measuring distances in space. For example: one **light year** is the distance travelled by light in one year. It is about 9 million million kilometres.

The nearest star to us (apart from the Sun) is Proxima Centauri. It is 4 light years away.

## Galaxies

The Sun is a member of a huge star system called a **galaxy**. This contains over 100 billion stars, and is nearly 100000 light years across. The galaxy is slowly rotating, and is held together by gravitational attraction.

Our galaxy is called the **Milky Way**. You can see the edge of its disc as a bright band of stars across the night sky. It is just one of many billions of galaxies in the known **Universe**.

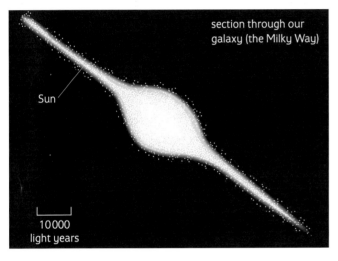

*Our own Sun is about halfway out from the centre of our galaxy.*

*The Andromeda galaxy is 2 million light years away. Its light has taken 2 million years to reach us.*

## Questions

1 What substance is the Sun mostly made of?
2 What substance does the Sun use as its nuclear fuel?
3 Explain what is meant by these terms:
   **a** galaxy  **b** Milky Way
   **c** constellation  **d** light year
4 Stars in the same constellation appear to form a group.
   Are they really in a group? If not, explain why not.
5 Write down an approximate value for each of these:
   **a** the distance travelled by light in one second.

**b** the number of stars in our galaxy.
**c** the diameter of our galaxy, in light years.
**d** how many times bigger the Sun's diameter is than the Earth's.
**e** the time taken for light to travel from the Sun to the Earth.
**f** the distance from Earth to the nearest star (apart from the Sun) in light years.
**g** the number of kilometres in a light year.
**h** the distance from Earth to the nearest star (apart from the Sun) in kilometres.

# The life of a star

The Sun is a rather average, middle-aged star. This is the story of how a star such as the Sun is born, how it shines, and how it dies.

## The birth of a star

Scientists think that the Sun and the rest of the Solar System formed about 4500 million years ago. It happened in a huge cloud of gas and dust called a **nebula**:

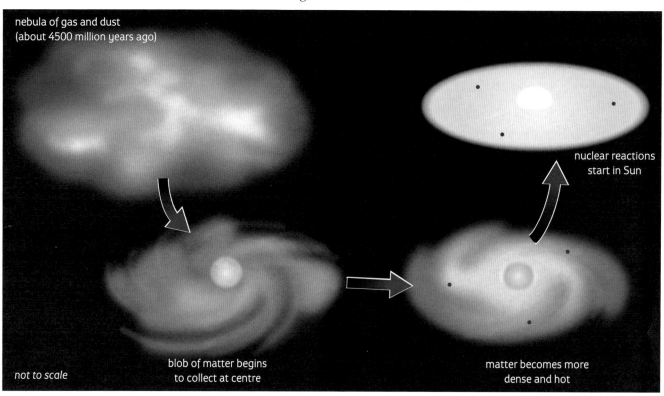

nebula of gas and dust
(about 4500 million years ago)

nuclear reactions
start in Sun

not to scale

blob of matter begins
to collect at centre

matter becomes more
dense and hot

In the nebula, gravity slowly pulled the gas and dust into blobs. In the centre, one blob grew bigger than all the rest. Around it, smaller blobs formed. Later, these would become planets and moons.

The Sun formed from the large blob in the centre. As gravity pulled in more and more material, the blob became hotter and hotter. Eventually, its core became so hot and compressed that nuclear reactions started, and the blob 'lit up' to become a star. Other stars formed – and are being formed – in the same way.

## Energy from a star

The Sun is 75% hydrogen gas. It uses hydrogen as its fuel. Deep in its core, nuclear reactions release vast amounts of energy from hydrogen by changing it into helium.

Scientists think that the Sun has enough hydrogen left in its core to keep it shining for another 6000 million years.

*The Great Nebula in the constellation of Orion. Stars are born in clouds of gas and dust such as this.*

## The death of a star

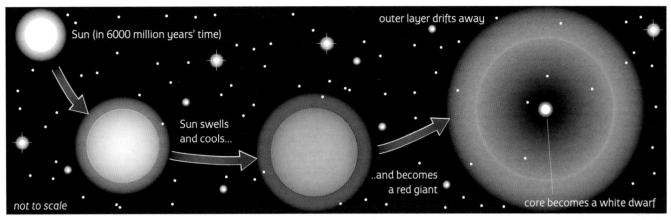

Sun (in 6000 million years' time)

outer layer drifts away

Sun swells and cools...

...and becomes a red giant

core becomes a white dwarf

not to scale

*The Crab Nebula: the remains of a supernova.*

In the Sun's core, the heating effect is so intense that it stops gravity pulling the material further inwards. However, in about 6000 million years' time, the core will have used up its hydrogen fuel, and will collapse. At the same time, the Sun's outer layer will expand and cool to a red glow. The Sun will have changed into a type of star called a **red giant**.

Eventually, the Sun's outer layer will drift into space, leaving a hot, dense core called a **white dwarf**. This tiny star will use helium as its fuel. When the helium runs out, the star will fade for ever.

## Supernovae and black holes

If a star is much more massive than the Sun, it dies a different death. It blows up in a gigantic nuclear explosion called a **supernova**, leaving a very dense core called a **neutron star**.

When the most massive stars of all explode, the core cannot resist the pull of gravity and goes on collapsing. The result is a **black hole**. Nothing can escape from a black hole, not even light. There may be a black hole at the centre of every galaxy.

## Questions

1 Like other stars, the Sun formed in a *nebula*.
  **a** What is a nebula?
  **b** What made matter in the nebula collect together in blobs?
  **c** About how long ago was the Sun formed?
  **d** What else formed in the nebula at the same time as the Sun?

2 The Sun gets its energy from nuclear reactions.
  **a** Where in the Sun do these reactions take place?
  **b** What fuel is the Sun using for these reactions?

  **c** About how long will it be before this fuel runs out?

3 One day, the Sun will become a *red giant*.
  **a** What is a red giant?
  **b** What will eventually happen to the Sun, after it has been a red giant?

4 **a** What is a *supernova*?
  **b** After a supernova has occurred, what is left at its centre?

## 11.18 Speedy delivery

## Making use of MASS

In American football, if your job is to charge through the defence lines, then you need as much mass as possible. The biggest players can have masses of over 120 kg. Once they start running, they are extremely difficult to stop.

The shot-putter below left needs mass as well as strength. When she pushes the shot forward, there is a backward push on her body which slows her down and reduces the speed of the shot. The more mass she has, the less effect this backward push has, and the better the throw.

## Who wins over 1500 metres?

In a race like the one below, swimmers would lose out because water resistance is much higher than air resistance. Cyclists are fastest of all, and even faster if there is another vehicle in front to reduce the air resistance. The highest speed ever reached on a bicycle was 63 metres per second (140 m.p.h.) – behind a car with a windshield on the back.

1.5 m/s    7 m/s    12 m/s    15 m/s

30 m.p.h.

# FAST SERVICE

Each image on this photograph was taken a fraction of a second after the previous one. Could you use the images to work out the speed of the racket? And if not, why not?

## Getting the elbow

A top tennis player uses a tightly strung racket to help her serve fast. She tries to hit the ball near the centre of the racket. Otherwise, the forces can injure her elbow. An ordinary player uses strings that are less tight. The strings stretch more when the ball is hit, which cuts the speed down. But, if the player hits the ball off-centre, the forces on the elbow are small and not so damaging.

## Talking points

Can you explain why:
● runners can travel faster than swimmers?
● cyclists can travel faster than runners?

See if you can find out how the following reduce the forces resisting their motion:

sprint cyclists    speed skaters    swimmers

Can you list the sports where having plenty of body mass is:

an advantage?    a disadvantage?

# 11.19

# g and more g

On Earth, if you drop something, it accelerates downwards at $10 \text{ m/s}^2$ (assuming no air resistance). In other words, its speed increases by 10 m/s every second. This is called the **acceleration of free fall**, or *g*. It is the same number as the Earth's gravitational field strength, also called *g*.

## *g* rides

Leisure park rides like this one give you the effects of high acceleration by making you travel round tight bends very fast. The maximum acceleration is about 3*g*.

High acceleration can drain blood from your head to your feet and make you 'black out'. But not during the ride below. Sitting with your knees up stops the rush of blood to your feet.

For the 5*g* ride on the left, you need skill and a million pounds worth of training. You also need a special 'g-suit'. During tight turns, parts of it inflate to squeeze your limbs and abdomen, so that the drain of blood from your head is reduced.

# The safest way to travel . . .

...is backwards, provided your seat has a high back.

Flying is already just about the safest form of travel there is. But if a plane has to make a crash landing, the deceleration can be very high. Rear-facing seats give the best chance of survival, which is why they are usually fitted in military transport aircraft. But so far, airlines haven't taken up the idea.

# High *g* performers

Some animals have evolved an amazing ability to withstand high *g* values:

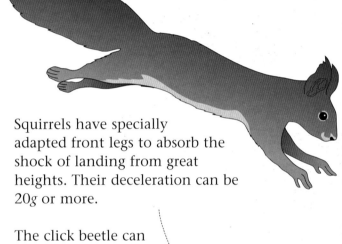

Squirrels have specially adapted front legs to absorb the shock of landing from great heights. Their deceleration can be 20*g* or more.

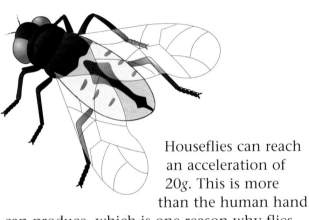

Houseflies can reach an acceleration of 20*g*. This is more than the human hand can produce, which is one reason why flies are so difficult to swat.

The click beetle can out-accelerate any other creature. It makes its escape by jack-knifing into the air with a peak acceleration of over 400*g*.

## Talking points

- In leisure park rides, you can experience accelerations of 3*g* or more. But without head restraints, accelerations like this wouldn't be safe. Can you explain why not?

- By using this book or other sources of information, see if you can find out what safety features cars have to reduce the acceleration or deceleration that passengers experience in a crash.

- If rear-facing seats are safer, can you suggest reasons why no airline has decided to 'go it alone' and fit them?

Scientists would love to find evidence of intelligent life out in space. They would be happy to find *any* form of life, even simple bacteria. But so far, their search is proving difficult.

## A home for life

The Earth is a special place. It has the rare conditions that make life possible, including liquid water, and a distance from the Sun which makes the temperature just right. It even has a big bodyguard, Jupiter, whose gravitational pull stops many comets and asteroids smashing into it.

But is Earth the only home for life? Within the Solar System, two other candidates are Mars and Europa – a moon of Jupiter. Mars seems to be a dead planet now, but water once flowed there, and simple life may have lived there. Europa has a warm interior and may have liquid water beneath its icy surface.

Living things change the land, sea, and air. For example, if life had not evolved on Earth, there would be much less oxygen in our atmosphere and no fossils in the rocks. So conditions on Mars and Europa may give clues about the existence of life there now or in the past.

Does life only exist on Earth?

... Or could it exist beneath the icy surface of Europa?

... Or on Mars? This wheeled robot found no evidence of life when it landed there. But future explorations might reveal something.

*Europa*

## SETI

Spacecraft can be sent to places in our Solar System, but a visit to even the nearest star would take thousands of years. If we want to detect life far out in space, we have to hope that the life is intelligent and sending out radio signals. The search for these signals is called the **SETI** project (the **Search for Extra-Terrestrial Intelligence**). It has been going on for over 40 years.

Radio telescopes like the one here are used to detect natural radio waves coming from stars. SETI scientists also use them to search for signals that might have been made by intelligent life.

If signals are ever found, communicating with their senders will be almost impossible. Radio waves take about 4 years to reach us from the nearest star, and 2 million years from our neighbouring galaxy, Andromeda. If we send signals now, it will be 2 million years before any Andromedans receive them.

# Little green men

In the late 1960s, the physicist Jocelyn Bell was analysing data from a radio telescope, when she noticed strange signals coming from a distant star. They were pulses so regular and rapid that, for a while, no one thought that they could be natural. Maybe the signals had been sent by distant aliens, or 'little green men' as they became known.

The **LGM (little green men)** theory was soon abandoned. What Jocelyn Bell had discovered was a new type of star called a **pulsar** – a rapidly spinning neutron star. It sends out radio beams whose pulses are rather like the flashes seen when a lighthouse beam sweeps round and round.

Maybe the next time strange pulses are found, they really will be coming from little green men.

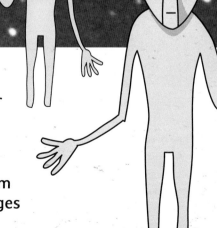

## Talking points

Can you explain why, in the immediate future, astronauts are unlikely to visit planets around other stars?

Can you explain what the SETI project is?

Can you explain why, if we pick up radio signals from distant aliens, we won't be able to exchange messages with them?

# Practice questions

**1** The graph below describes the motion of a bus as it travels from village to village.

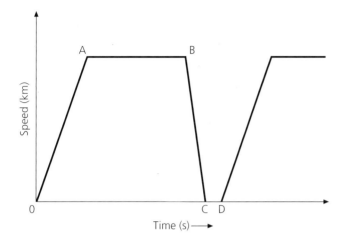

**i** Describe in detail what is happening between OA, AB, BC and CD.

**ii** Sketch an acceleration/time graph for the bus's journey.

**2** Emma and Jane are having a race. The graph below shows how the speed of each athlete changes with time.

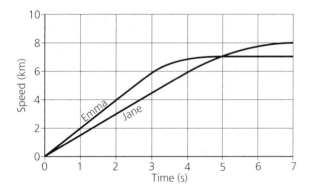

**a** Which athlete reaches the higher speed?

**b** Which athelete has the greater acceleration at the start of the race?

**c** After how many seconds does Jane's speed become greater than Emma's?

**d** What is Emma's maximum speed?

**e** To begin with, Emma's acceleration is $2\,m/s^2$. What does this figure tell you about the way her speed changes?

**3** The table below shows how the stopping distance of a car depends on its speed.

| Stopping distance (m) | 0 | 4 | 12 | 22 | 36 | 52 | 72 |
|---|---|---|---|---|---|---|---|
| Speed (m/s) | 0 | 5 | 10 | 15 | 20 | 25 | 30 |

**a** Write down TWO factors, apart from speed, that affect the stopping distance of a car.

**b** Use the information in the above table to draw a graph of stopping distance against speed.

**c** The speed limit in a housing estate is 12.5m/s.
Use your graph to estimate the stopping distance of a car travelling at this speed.

**d** Describe how the stopping distance changes as the speed of a car increases.

**4** The diagram below shows a bobsleigh team at the beginning of their run.

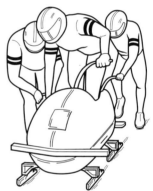

**a** When the team push the bobsleigh the forces they apply cause it to accelerate. Name one place where the team need **i** a large amount of friction and **ii** as small amount of friction as possible.

**b** What do the team do on their way down the run to reduce any resistive forces?

**c** Why do the team need a lot of friction at the end of the run?

**5** In each of the following cases, decide whether the frictional forces should be as *low* as possible or as *high* as possible:

**a** Shoes in contact with the pavement.

**b** Brake blocks being pressed against the rim of a bicycle wheel.

**c** Hands holding the handlebars of a bicycle.

**d** Skis sliding over snow.

**e** Car tyres in contact with a road surface.

**f** A wheel turning on its axle.

156

**6** Copy and complete the following sentences.

**a i** When a stone is dropped it falls to the ground. The force causing this is called _____. As the stone falls its speed _____.

**ii** We measure forces in units called _____.

**iii** Before the stone was dropped it had _____ energy. Just before it hit the ground this had all changed into _____ energy.

**b** A crate weighing 1000 N is lifted a vertical distance of 2 m. Calculate the work done on the crate.

**7** A lead ball and a feather are held at the same height above the ground and then released together.

**a** Which object hits the ground first? Explain your answer.

**b** Why do shuttlecraft which are returning from orbiting the Earth release 'drag chutes' just after they have landed?

**8 a** A car accelerates from 0 to 200 km/h in 20 s. What is the average acceleration of this car? Why is this *average* acceleration?

**b** A train slows down from 120 km/h to 40 km/h in 20 s. What is the deceleration of the train? What is the acceleration of the train?

**c** A small rocket on bonfire night accelerates from rest to 40 m/s in 4 s. What is the acceleration of the rocket?

**9** A skydiver falls from a hovering helicopter. She waits a few seconds before opening her parachute. The table below shows how her speed changes with time from the moment she jumps:

| Time (s) | 0 | 1 | 2 | 3 | 4 | 5 | 6 | 7 | 8 |
|---|---|---|---|---|---|---|---|---|---|
| Speed (m/s) | 0 | | 20 | 30 | 22 | 14 | 12 | 9 | 9 |

**a** Copy and complete the table, filling in the missing number.

**b** Plot a graph of speed against time.

**c** After how many seconds does the skydiver open her parachute? How can you tell from your graph?

**d** As the skydiver falls, there is a *downward* force acting on her and an *upward* force.

**i** What causes the downward force?

**ii** What causes the upward force?

**iii** After 2 seconds, which of these two forces is the larger?

**iv** After 8 seconds, how do the two forces compare?

**e** How would you expect your graph to be different if the skydiver's parachute were larger? (You could answer this by drawing sketches to show how the graph changes.)

**10** Copy and complete the sentences below choosing words from this list:

**Galaxy planet satellite constellation star**

**a** The Sun is a _____.

**b** The moon is a natural _____.

**c** A small group of stars, as seen from the Earth, is called a _____.

**d** The Milky Way is the name of our _____.

**11**

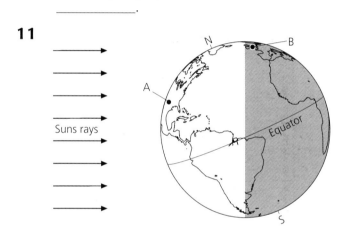

**a** Explain why it is daytime at A.

**b** Explain why it is night-time at B.

**c** How long does it take for the Earth to complete one rotation?

**d** The Earth has one natural satellite. What is it called?

**e** What forces keep the Earth in orbit around the Sun?

**f** Mercury and Venus are two planets that are closer to the Sun than the Earth. Are the forces they experience larger or smaller than those experienced by the Earth? Explain your answer.

**12a** Name one luminous object in the night sky.

**b** Name one non-luminous object in the night sky.

**c** The diagrams show the constellation Taurus on two nights a month apart.

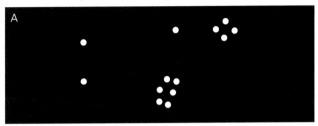

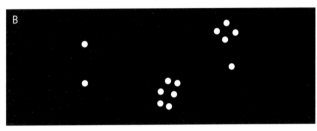

**i** What evidence is there that one of the objects is a planet? Make a sketch to show which object it is.

**ii** Why will the planet not always appear to be among the stars of Taurus?

**d i** What is a satellite?

**ii** Name one artificial satellite.

**13** The diagram below shows two identical satellites, A and B, in orbit around the Earth.

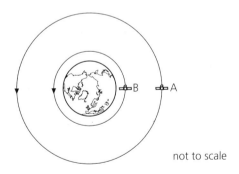

not to scale

**a** Which satellite is pulled most strongly by the Earth's gravitational field?

**b** Which satellite has the highest speed?

**c** Which satellite will take longest to complete one orbit of the Earth?

**d** Satellite A is in a geostationary orbit. What does this mean?

**e** Why are communications satellites normally put into geostationary orbits?

**14** The diagram shows the path of a satellite placed in a low polar orbit round the Earth.

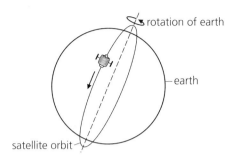

It takes the above satellite 2 hours to orbit the Earth.

**a** How many orbits will the satellite complete in one full day?

**b** Explain why a low polar orbit is useful for weather satellites.

**c** Describe one other use for a satellite in this kind of orbit.

**d** Why would this kind of orbit be no use for a communications satellite?

**e** What is a geostationary orbit?

**15** Here is some data about the planets:

| Planet | Diameter of planet in km | Average distance from Sun in million km | Time for one orbit in years | Average surface temperature in °C |
|--------|------|------|------|------|
| Mercury | 4900 | 58 | 0.2 | 350 |
| Venus | 12 000 | 108 | 0.6 | 480 |
| Earth | 12 800 | 150 | 1.0 | 22 |
| Mars | 6800 | 228 | 1.9 | −23 |
| Jupiter | 143 000 | 778 | 11.9 | −150 |
| Saturn | 120 000 | 1427 | 29.5 | −180 |
| Uranus | 52 000 | 2870 | 84.0 | −210 |
| Neptune | 49 000 | 4497 | 164.8 | −220 |
| Pluto | 3000 | 5900 | 247.8 | −230 |

Use the above table to answer the following questions.

**a** Which is the largest planet?

**b** Which is the smallest planet?

**c** Which planet is closest to the Sun?

**d** Which planet takes almost twelve earth years to orbit the Sun?

**e** How long is a year on the planet Mercury? Explain your answer.

**f** How would you expect a planet's surface temperature to depend on its distance from the Sun? Does the data in the above table support this? Explain your answer.

**16** The graph below shows the orbit times and average distance from the Sun for several planets.

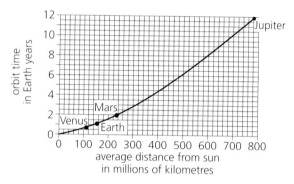

**a** Which planet experiences the largest gravitational forces from the Sun?

**b** Which planet experiences the smallest gravitational forces from the Sun?

**c** Explain why Jupiter takes longer to orbit the Sun than Venus.

**d** Between which planets is the asteroid belt?

**e** Estimate the orbit time for an asteroid in the middle of the belt.

**f** What is the shape of the orbits of the planets and the asteroids?

**17** The diagram shows the orbit of a comet.

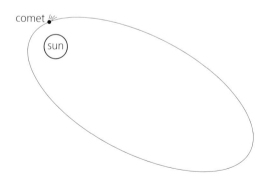

**a** What is a comet?

**b** What is the shape of a comet's orbit?

**c** Where in a comet's orbit is it moving the slowest? Explain your answer.

**18** meteorite     galaxy     supernova

big bang     constellation     black hole

moon comet     Solar System

Which of the above is the best match for each of the following descriptions?

**a** A rocky object orbiting a planet.

**b** The Sun, its planets, and other objects in orbit.

**c** A small rocky object which collides with a planet, and may be a fragment from an asteroid.

**d** A clump of ice, gas, and dust, usually in a highly elliptical orbit around the Sun.

**e** A huge group of many millions of stars.

**f** A gigantic explosion that occurs when a very massive star has used up its nuclear fuel.

**19** The Sun is a star. It formed in a nebula about 4 500 million years ago. The diagram below shows what is likely to happen to the Sun in about 6 000 million years' time.

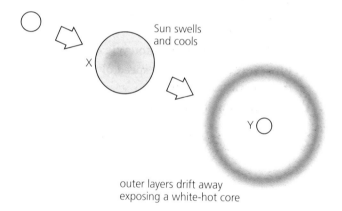

**a** What is a nebula?

**b** What makes matter in a nebula collect together to form a star?

**c** The Sun gets its energy from nuclear reactions that change hydrogen into helium. What is this process called?

**d** What type of star has the Sun become at X in the diagram above?

**e** What type of star is left when the core, Y, is exposed?

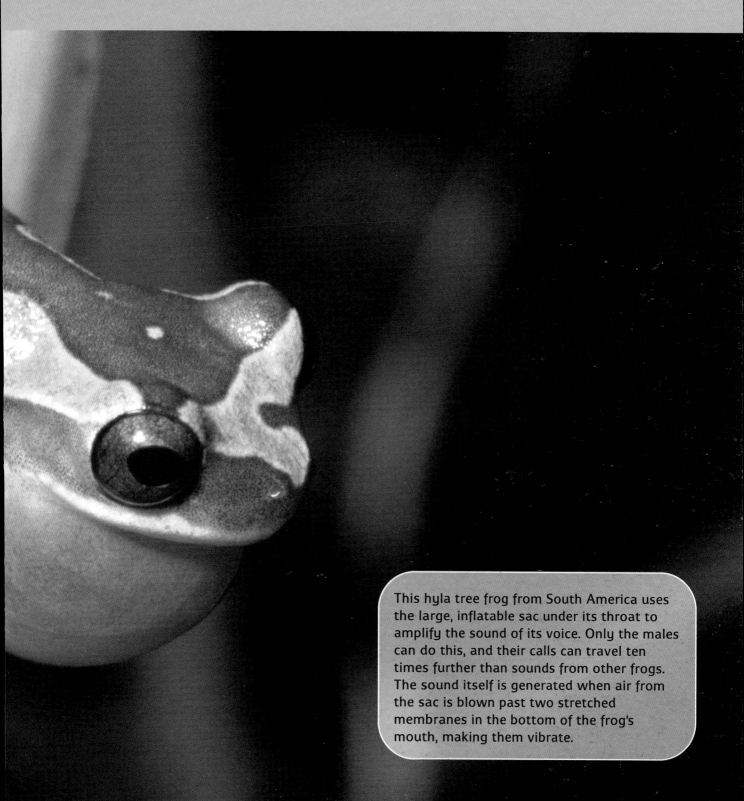

# Module 12

This hyla tree frog from South America uses the large, inflatable sac under its throat to amplify the sound of its voice. Only the males can do this, and their calls can travel ten times further than sounds from other frogs. The sound itself is generated when air from the sac is blown past two stretched membranes in the bottom of the frog's mouth, making them vibrate.

# Moving waves

If you drop a stone into a pond, tiny waves spread across the surface, as shown in the photograph above. The moving wave effect is the result of up-and-down motions in the water.

Light, sound, and radio signals all travel in the form of waves. Waves carry energy from one place to another, but without any material being transferred.

There are two main types of wave. You can demonstrate them with a 'slinky' spring as shown below. When a coil **oscillates** (moves to and fro), it makes the next one oscillate a fraction of a second later... and so on. This produces the moving wave effect.

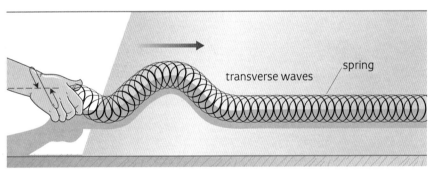

**Transverse waves** have oscillations which are from side to side (or up and down). Light and radio waves travel like this.

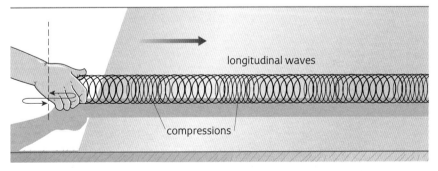

**Longitudinal waves** have oscillations which are backwards and forwards. Sound waves travel like this.

**Did you know?**

**How to draw waves**

Transverse waves can be drawn as shown above.

You can also draw waves using lines called wavefronts. Think of each wavefront as the top of a transverse wave, or the compression of a longitudinal wave.

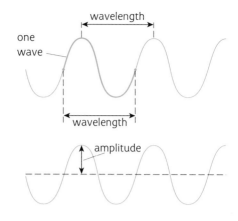

one wave — wavelength

wavelength

amplitude

# Describing waves

Imagine some waves travelling across water. Here are some of the terms used when describing them:

**Speed** This is measured in metres per second (m/s).

**Frequency** This is the number of waves sent out per second. It is measured in hertz (Hz). For example, if 3 waves are sent out every second, the frequency is 3 Hz.

**Wavelength** This is the distance from one point on a wave to the matching point on the next wave.

**Amplitude** This is the distance shown in the diagram .

**Period** This is the time between one wave peak and the next. For example, if 3 waves are sent out every second, the time between one wave peak and the next is $\frac{1}{3}$ second. So the period is $\frac{1}{3}$ second.

# An equation for waves

Speed, frequency, and wavelength are linked by an equation. The panel below shows why it works:

$$\underset{\text{in m/s}}{\text{speed}} \quad = \quad \underset{\text{in Hz}}{\text{frequency}} \times \underset{\text{in m}}{\text{wavelength}}$$

**Did you know?**

**High frequencies**

1 **kilohertz** (kHz) = 1000 Hz
(one thousand waves per second)

1 **megahertz** (MHz) = 1000 000 Hz
(one million waves per second)

---

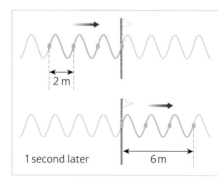

2 m

1 second later        6 m

3 waves pass the flag in one second...    ...so the frequency is 3 Hz.
Each wave is 2 metres long...            ...so the wavelength is 2 m.

This means that:

the waves travel 6 metres in one second...    ...so the speed is 6 m/s.

Therefore:       6 m/s    =    3 Hz    ×    2 m
                (speed)      (frequency)    (wavelength)

---

## Questions

**1** What is the difference between *longitudinal waves* and *transverse waves*?

**2** Three waves have the *same speed*, but different frequencies and wavelengths. Copy the table to the right, and fill in the blank spaces.

|  | Speed in m/s | Frequency in Hz | Wavelength in m |
|---|---|---|---|
| wave 1 |  | 8 | 4 |
| wave 2 |  | 16 |  |
| wave 3 |  |  | 1 |

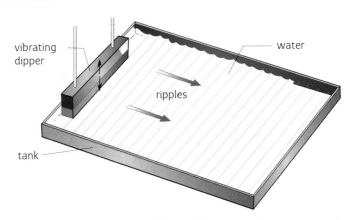

You can use a **ripple tank** like the one above to study how waves behave. Ripples (tiny waves) are sent across the surface of the water, towards different obstacles. Here are some of the effects produced.

## Reflection

A vertical barrier is put in the path of the waves. The waves are reflected from the barrier at the same angle as they strike it.

## Refraction

A flat piece of plastic makes the water more shallow. This slows the waves down. When they slow, they change direction. This bending effect is called **refraction**.

## Diffraction

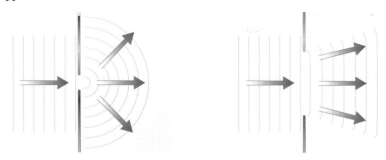

Waves bend round obstacles, or spread as they pass through gaps. This is called **diffraction**. It works best if the width of the gap is about the same as the wavelength. Wider gaps cause less diffraction.

## Wave evidence

Sound, light, and radio signals can be reflected, refracted, and diffracted. This is evidence that they travel as waves. Sound waves diffract round large obstacles, which is why you can hear round corners. Light waves are much shorter, so gaps have to be very tiny to diffract them.

## Questions

1 Write down whether each of the following is an example of *reflection*, *refraction*, or *diffraction*.

   **a** A beam of light bouncing off a mirror, as in photograph X on the right.

   **b** A beam of light bending on entering a glass block, as in photograph Y on the right.

   **c** Sound bending round a wall, so that you can hear someone speaking on the other side.

   **d** Radio waves bending round a hill, so that a radio can still pick up signals down in a valley.

2 In the diagram on the right, waves are moving towards a harbour wall.

   **a** What will happen to waves striking the harbour wall at A?

   **b** What will happen to waves slowed by the submerged sandbank at B?

   **c** What will happen to waves passing through the harbour entrance at C?

   **d** If the harbour entrance were wider, what difference would this make?

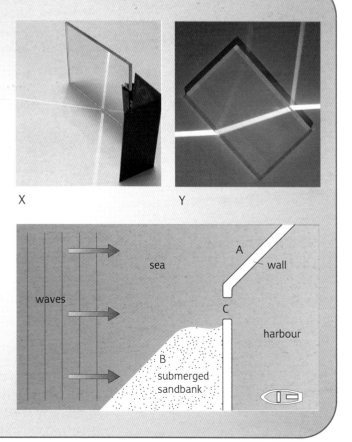

# Rays of light

Light is a form of radiation. This just means that light radiates (spreads out) from its source. In diagrams, lines called **rays** are used to show which way the light is going.

On Earth, the Sun is our main source of light.

*If you can see a beam of light, this is because tiny particles of dust, smoke, or mist are reflecting some of the light into your eyes.*

## Questions

1 Give *two* examples of things that give off their own light.

2 Give *two* examples of things that can only be seen because they reflect light from another source.

You see some things because they give off their own light. The Sun, lamps, lasers, and glowing TV screens are like this.

You see other things because daylight, or other light, bounces off them. They **reflect** light, and some goes into your eyes. That is why you can see this page. The white paper reflects light well, so it looks bright. However, the black letters **absorb** light and reflect very little. That is why they look so dark. Transparent materials like glass and water let light pass right through them. They **transmit** light.

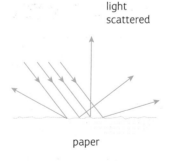

light scattered

paper

Irregular reflection

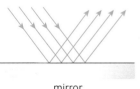

mirror

Regular reflection

black surface

Absorption

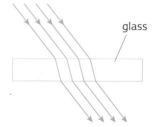

glass

Transmission

Most surfaces are uneven, or contain materials that scatter light. They reflect light in all directions. In other words, the reflection is *irregular*. Mirrors are smooth and shiny. When they reflect light, the reflection is *regular*.

## Features of light

**Light travels in straight lines** You can see this if you look at the path of a sunbeam or a laser beam.

**Light travels as waves** The 'ripples' can't be seen. They are tiny, vibrating electric and magnetic forces. The waves are transverse – their vibrations are the up-and-down type. They are also very small: more than 2000 light waves would fit into a millimetre.

To explain some effects, scientists find it useful to think of light as a stream of tiny 'energy particles'. They call them **photons**.

**Light can travel through a vacuum (empty space)** Electric and magnetic ripples do not need a material to travel through. That is why light can reach us from the Sun and stars.

**Light is the fastest thing there is** In space, the speed of light is 300 000 kilometres per second. Nothing can travel faster than this. The speed of light seems to be a universal speed limit.

**Light delivers energy** Energy is needed to produce light. Materials gain energy when they absorb light. For example, solar cells use the energy in sunlight to produce electricity.

*Light from a laser.*

*This solar-powered car uses the energy in sunlight to produce electricity for its motor.*

## Questions

**3** Which of the materials below would you expect to:
**a** mainly reflect light? **b** mainly absorb light?
**c** mainly transmit light?
(There may be more than one answer to each part.)

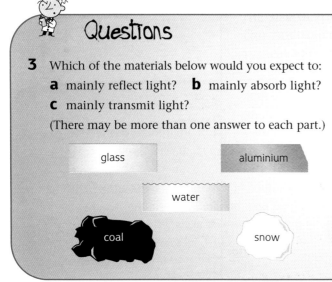

glass · aluminium · water · coal · snow

**4** Give one piece of evidence that light waves can travel through a vacuum (empty space).

**5** Give one piece of evidence that light delivers energy.

**6** Give *two* pieces of evidence that light travels in straight lines.

**7** Light is the fastest thing there is.
   **a** What is the speed of light? (You will find the information somewhere on this page.)
   **b** If the Moon is 384 000 km from Earth, will light from the Moon take *less* than one second to reach the Earth, or *more* than one second?

# Bending light

In the 'broken pencil' illusion below left, the glass block bends the light as it enters and leaves it. The bending effect is called refraction. Water and other transparent materials also refract light, though by different amounts.

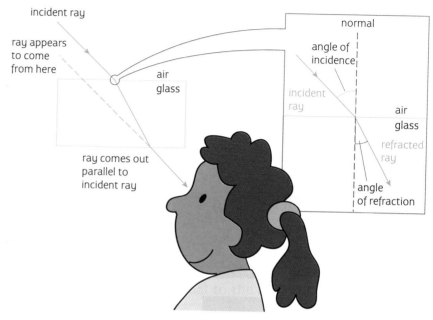

The 'broken pencil' illusion is caused by the refraction (bending) of light.

The diagram above shows how a ray passes through a glass block. The line at right-angles to the side of the block is called the **normal**. The ray is refracted towards the normal when it enters the block, and away from the normal when it leaves it.

With a rectangular block like the one above, the ray comes out parallel to its original direction. If the ray strikes the block at right-angles ('square on'), it goes straight through without being refracted.

## Deeper than it looks

Because of refraction, water looks less deep than it really is. The diagram below shows why this happens.

## Questions

1 A glass block can bend light. What name is given to the bending effect?

2 In the photograph above, why does the middle of the pen appear to be moved to one side?

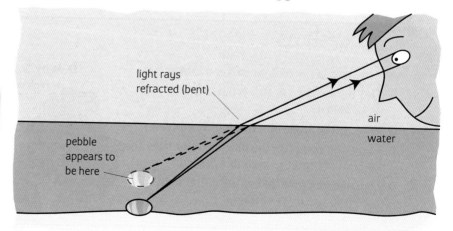

When rays from the pebble leave the water, they are refracted. To the viewer, they seem to come from a point that is higher, and closer. This effect makes objects look larger underwater. When scientists or archaeologists are working on marine life or wrecks, they tend to overestimate sizes and must measure for accuracy.

## Forming a spectrum

*Red light is refracted (bent) the least by a prism, and violet light the most. However, in this diagram, the difference has been exaggerated (it has been made to look bigger than it really is).*

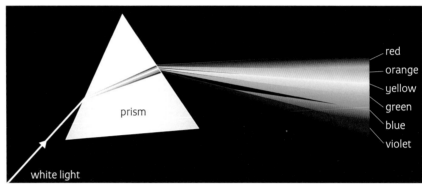

A **prism** is a triangular block of glass or plastic. When a narrow beam of white light passes through a prism, the beam splits into all the colours of the rainbow. That is because white isn't a single colour, but a mixture of colours. The colours enter the prism together but are refracted (bent) different amounts by the glass. The effect is called **dispersion**.

*Raindrops can act like tiny prisms when sunlight strikes them.*

The range of colours is called a **spectrum**. Most people think they can see six colours. However, the spectrum is really a continuous change of colour from beginning to end.

The different colours in the spectrum are actually light waves of different wavelengths. Red light has the longest wavelength, violet the shortest.

## Questions

**3 a** Copy the diagram on the right. Draw in and label the *normal* and the *refracted ray*.

**b** Redraw the diagram to show what happens to a ray of light if it strikes the glass at right-angles ('square on').

**4** When a narrow beam of white light passes through a prism, it spreads out into a range of colours.

**a** What is this range of colours called?

**b** Which colour is refracted (bent) most by a prism?

**c** Which colour is refracted least?

**5** Why does water look less deep than it really is?

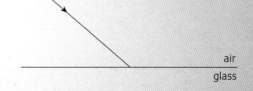

# Internal reflections

**Objectives**

**This spread should help you to**
- explain what total internal reflection is, and give some examples of its use

The inside surface of water, glass, or other transparent materials can act like a perfect mirror.

The diagrams below show what happens to three rays leaving an underwater lamp at different angles. If light strikes the surface at a angle greater than the **critical angle**, there is no refracted ray. All the light is reflected. The effect is called **total internal reflection**.

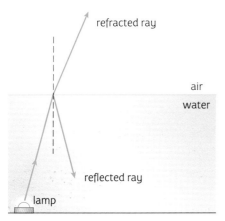

*The ray splits into a refracted ray and a weaker reflected ray.*

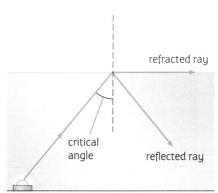

*The ray splits, but the refracted ray only just leaves the surface.*

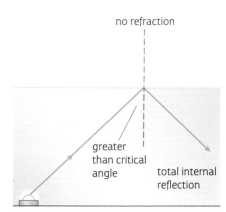

*There is no refracted ray. The surface of the water acts like a perfect mirror.*

|  | Critical angles |
|---|---|
| water | 49° |
| acrylic plastic | 42° |
| glass | 41° |

The value of the critical angle depends on the material, as you can see in the table on the left.

## Reflecting prisms

Total internal reflection can take place inside a prism. In the examples below, the prisms are made of glass or acrylic plastic.

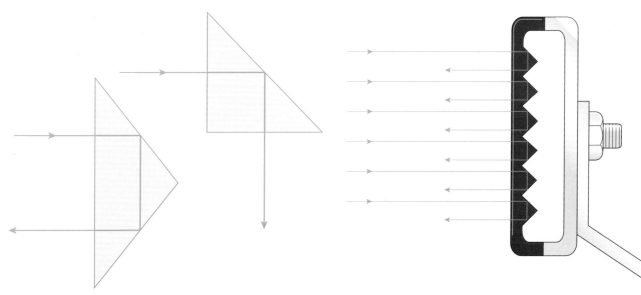

*The inside faces of these prisms act like perfect mirrors because the light is striking them at 45°. That is bigger than the critical angle for glass or acrylic plastic.*

*The rear reflectors on cars and cycles contain lots of tiny prisms. These use total internal reflection to send light back in the opposite direction.*

## Optical fibres

**Optical fibres** are very thin, flexible rods of glass (or transparent plastic). They use total internal reflection. Light put in at one end is reflected from side to side until it comes out of the other end, as shown below.

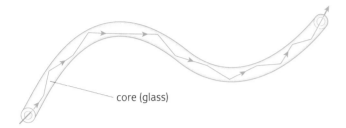

core (glass)

*A single optical fibre. In the type shown here, the core has a coating around it to protect its reflecting surface.*

*A bundle of optical fibres. If the fibres are in matching positions at both ends, you can see a picture through them.*

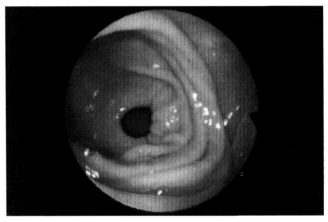

*A group of optical fibres. Telephone calls can be carried by optical fibres. The signals are coded and sent along the fibre as pulses of laser light.*

*This photograph was taken through an **endoscope**, an instrument used by surgeons for looking inside the body. An endoscope contains a long, thin bundle of optical fibres.*

## Questions

1  Copy and complete the diagrams right to show where each ray goes after it strikes the prism.

2  When light goes into one end of an optical fibre, why does it all come out of the other end, with none escaping from the sides?

3  **a** Give *two* examples of the practical use of optical fibres.

   **b** Give one more example of the practical use of total internal reflection.

4  Glass's critical angle is 41°. What does this mean?

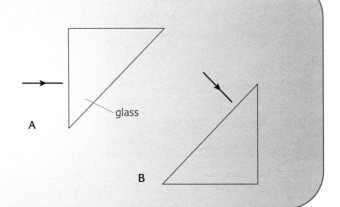

glass

A

B

## 12.07 Electromagnetic waves

### Objectives

**This spread should help you to**

- describe the different types of electromagnetic wave, and their effects and uses

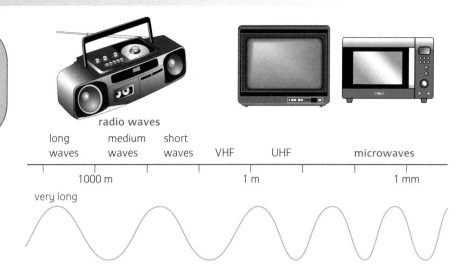

*The different types of electromagnetic wave. They are sometimes called electromagnetic radiation because they radiate (spread out) from their source.*

*A microwave aerial for satellite TV.*

*A hot, glowing material like this is giving off a mixture of visible red light and invisible infrared.*

Light is a member of a whole family of waves called the **electromagnetic spectrum**.

**Radio waves** These are produced by making a current vibrate in an aerial. They can be sent out in a special pattern which tells a radio or TV what sounds or pictures to make.

Long and medium waves are used for AM radio.

VHF (very high frequency) waves are used for high-quality FM stereo radio.

UHF (ultra high frequency) waves are used for terrestrial TV.

**Microwaves** These are radio waves of very short wavelength. They are used for satellite communication, beaming television and telephone signals round the country, and mobile phone networks. They are also used for radar.

Some microwaves are absorbed strongly by food. Their energy makes the food hot. Microwave ovens make use of this idea.

**Infrared** Hot things like fires all give off infrared radiation. In fact, everything gives off some infrared. If you absorb it, it heats you up.

As objects get hotter, the infrared wavelengths they give off get shorter. When something is 'red hot', some wavelengths are so short that they can be picked up by the eye.

TV remote controllers send instructions using infrared pulses.

**Light** This is the only part of the spectrum which the eye can detect.

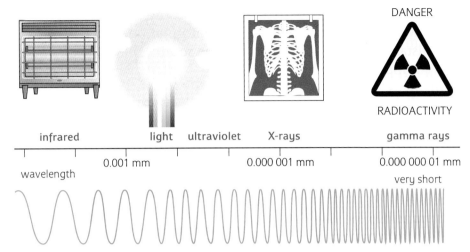

DANGER

RADIOACTIVITY

infrared     light   ultraviolet    X-rays      gamma rays

0.001 mm      0.000 001 mm     0.000 000 01 mm

wavelength                                        very short

*Features of electromagnetic waves*
- *They carry energy.*
- *They can travel through empty space.*
- *Their speed through space (and air) is 300 000 km/s. This is called the* **speed of light**, *although they all travel at this speed.*

*The Sun's ultraviolet radiation causes tanning – and skin cancer.*

**Ultraviolet** This is present in sunlight, although your eyes can't detect it. It is the type of radiation that produces a sun tan. But too much can cause skin cancer, and damage your eyes.

Some chemicals glow when they absorb ultraviolet. The effect is called **fluorescence**. In fluorescent lamps, the inside of the tube is coated with a white powder which glows and gives off light when it absorbs ultraviolet from 'electrified' gas in the tube.

**X-rays** Shorter wavelengths can penetrate dense metals. Longer wavelengths can pass through flesh, but not bone. So they can be used to take 'shadow' photographs of bones. Only brief bursts are allowed because X-rays can damage living cells and cause cancer.

**Gamma rays** These come from radioactive materials and have the same effects as X-rays. They can be used for sterilizing medical instruments, because they kill germs. Concentrated beams of gamma rays (or X-rays) can be used to kill cancer cells.

## Questions

1  The chart at the top of the page shows the different types of electromagnetic wave. Give *two* features that all the waves in the chart have.

2  Write down which of the electromagnetic waves are described by each of the following (in some cases, there may be more than one type):

   **a** can be detected by the eye.

   **b** can pass right through flesh.

   **c** have the longest wavelength.

   **d** are used for radar.

   **e** are given off by warm objects.

   **f** are given off by red-hot objects.

   **g** are used for cooking.

   **h** cause sun-tanning in some types of skin.

   **i** can damage living cells deep in the body.

   **j** are sent out in pulses by TV remote controllers.

   **k** are used for communications.

   **l** cause chemicals to glow in fluorescent lamps.

# Sound waves

**Objectives**

**This spread should help you to**

- describe what sound waves are and how they travel

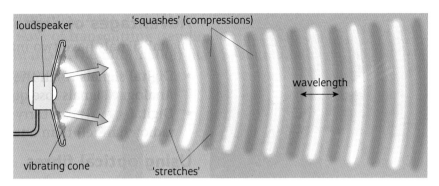

When the cone of a loudspeaker vibrates, it moves in and out very fast, stretching and squashing the air in front of it. The 'stretches' and 'squashes' spread through the air – rather as ripples spread across a pond. They are **sound waves**. When they reach your ears, they make your eardrums vibrate and you hear a **sound**.

The 'squashes' are **compressions**. Here, the air pressure is higher than normal. Diagrams often show compressions as lines.

## Features of sound

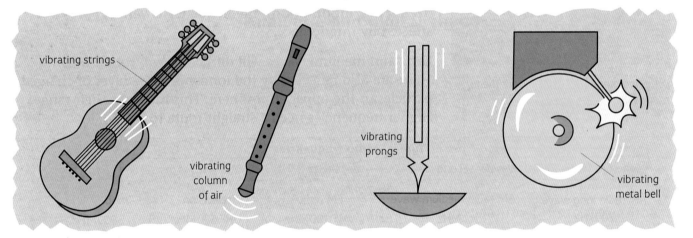

**Sound waves are caused by vibrations** Any vibrating object can be a source of sound waves. The cone of a loudspeaker is one example. There are some more above.

**Sound waves are longitudinal waves** This means that their vibrations are backwards and forwards, rather than up and down like ripples.

**Sound waves can be reflected and refracted** There is more about this in the next spread.

**Sound waves can be diffracted** This means that they can bend round obstacles and through gaps. That is why you can hear round corners.

**Questions**

1 In sound waves, what is the distance between compressions called?

2 How are sound waves different from the ripples that spread across water?

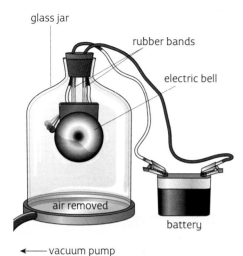

glass jar

rubber bands

electric bell

air removed

battery

← vacuum pump

*If the air is removed from the jar, the bell can't be heard.*

**Did you know?**

The waveform on the right looks like a series of waves. But it is really a graph of pressure against time. It shows how the air pressure near the microphone rises and falls as sound waves pass.

**Sound waves can travel through solids, liquids, and gases**

Most sounds reaching the ear have travelled through air. But you also hear sounds underwater. Walls, windows, doors, and ceilings can also transmit (pass on) sound.

**Sound waves can't travel through a vacuum (empty space)**

If the air is pumped out of the jar on the left, the sound stops, though the bell goes on working. Sound waves can't be made if there's no material to squash and stretch.

## Seeing sounds

You can't actually see sounds. But with an **oscilloscope** connected to a **microphone**, you can show sounds as wave shapes on a screen.

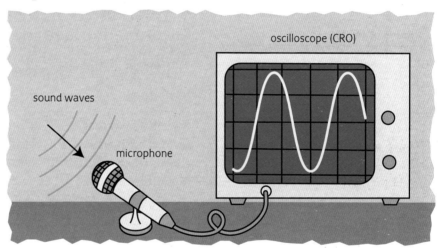

oscilloscope (CRO)

sound waves

microphone

When sound waves go into the microphone, the vibrations are changed into electrical signals. The oscilloscope uses these to make a spot vibrate up and down on the screen. It moves it steadily sideways at the same time. The result is called a **waveform**.

## Questions

**3**  *compressions*     *vibrations*     *waveforms*

Choose the word above which goes with each of the following:

**a** Sound waves are caused by these.

**b** In sound waves, these are regions of higher pressure.

**4** Give one piece of evidence that shows each of the following:

**a** Sound can travel through a gas.

**b** Sound can travel through a liquid.

**c** Sound can travel through a solid.

**d** Sound cannot travel through a vacuum.

**5** Give a reason for each of the following:

**a** Sound cannot travel through a vacuum.

**b** It is possible to hear round corners.

**6** Sound waves are longitudinal waves – their vibrations are backwards-and-forwards. Why are transverse (up-and-down) 'waves' seen on the screen of the oscilloscope when someone whistles into the microphone?

# Speed of sound and echoes

## Objectives

**This spread should help you to**
- describe how fast sound travels
- explain how echoes are produced

*Sound is much slower than light, so you hear lightning after you see it.*

Speed of sound in ...

| | |
|---|---|
| air at 0°C | 330 m/s |
| air at 30°C | 350 m/s |
| water at 0°C | 1400 m/s |
| concrete | 5000 m/s |

## The speed of sound

In air, the speed of sound is about 330 metres per second (760 m.p.h.), although this can vary depending on the temperature.

Sound takes about 3 seconds to travel one kilometre. Light does it almost in an instant. So, if you see lightning, then hear the crash 3 seconds later, the lightning must be about a kilometre away.

Sound travels faster in liquids than in gases (such as air). It travels fastest of all in solids. There are some examples on the left.

## Refraction of sound

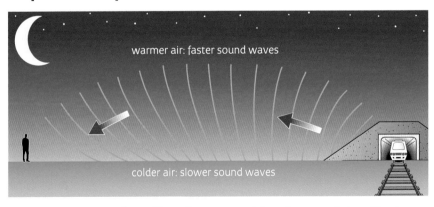

warmer air: faster sound waves

colder air: slower sound waves

Distant trains and traffic often sound louder at night. During the night-time, when the ground cools quickly, air near the ground becomes colder than that above. Sound waves travel more slowly through this colder air. So waves leaving the ground tend to bend back towards it, instead of spreading upwards. The bending effect is called **refraction**.

## Questions

1 Why do you hear lightning after you see it?

2 If their speed changes, sound waves may change direction. What is this effect called?

## Reflection of sound: echoes

Hard surfaces such as walls reflect sound waves. When you hear an **echo**, you are hearing a reflected sound a short time after the original sound.

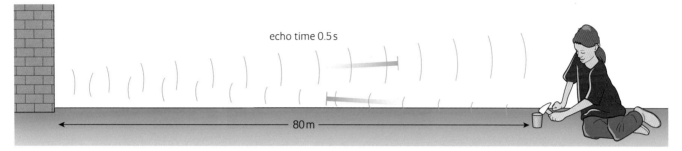

echo time 0.5 s

80 m

Above, the girl is 80 metres from a large brick wall. Every time she hits the block of wood, she hears an echo 0.5 seconds later. This is the echo time. It is the time taken for the sound to travel the 160 metres to the wall *and back again*.

Now you can work out a value for the speed of sound:

$$\text{speed of sound} = \frac{\text{distance travelled}}{\text{time taken}} = \frac{\text{distance to wall and back}}{\text{echo time}}$$

So:

$$\text{speed of sound} = \frac{160}{0.5} = 320 \text{ metres/second (m/s)}$$

If you measure an echo time, but already know the speed of sound, you can work out how far away the reflecting surface is. This is the idea behind the **echo-sounders** which ships use to measure depth. You can find out more about them in the spread on **Ultrasound**.

## Questions

*Assume that the speed of sound in air is 330 m/s.*

**3** Which of the things in the chart below is travelling faster than sound does in air?

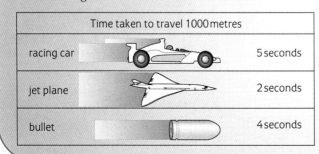

| Time taken to travel 1000 metres | | |
|---|---|---|
| racing car | | 5 seconds |
| jet plane | | 2 seconds |
| bullet | | 4 seconds |

**4** If lightning strikes, and you hear it 4 seconds after you see it, how far away is it?

**5** Which does sound travel faster through:

   **a** *cold air* or *warm air*?

   **b** *a solid* or *a gas*?

**6** A ship is 330 metres from a large cliff when it sounds its foghorn.

   **a** When the echo is heard on the ship, how far has the sound travelled?

   **b** What is the echo time (the time delay before the echo is heard)?

# High and low, loud and quiet

**Objectives**

**This spread should help you to**

- describe how high sounds differ from low ones, and loud sounds from quiet ones
- use the wave equation

He sings louder than her. He creates bigger vibrations in the air. But she can reach higher notes than him. She can give out more sound waves every second.

## Frequency and pitch

The **frequency** of a sound is measured in hertz (Hz). If a loudspeaker cone vibrates 100 times per second, it gives out 100 sound waves per second, and the frequency is 100 Hz.

Different frequencies sound different to the ear. You hear *high* frequencies as *high* notes: they have a **high pitch**. You hear *low* frequencies as *low* notes: they have a **low pitch**. So:

The higher the frequency of a sound, the higher its pitch.

The human ear can detect frequencies ranging from about 20 Hz up to 20 000 Hz, although the upper limit gets less with age.

Below, you can see what different frequencies look like on the screen of an oscilloscope. With the higher frequency, there are more waves on the screen: the waves are closer together.

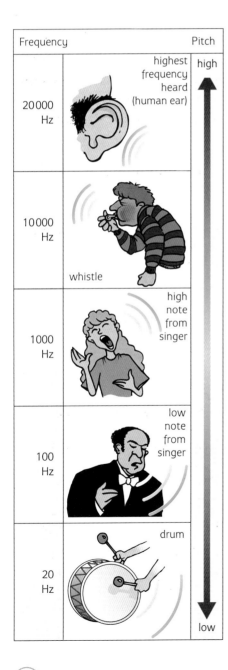

| Frequency | | Pitch |
|---|---|---|
| 20 000 Hz | highest frequency heard (human ear) | high |
| 10 000 Hz | whistle | |
| 1000 Hz | high note from singer | |
| 100 Hz | low note from singer | |
| 20 Hz | drum | low |

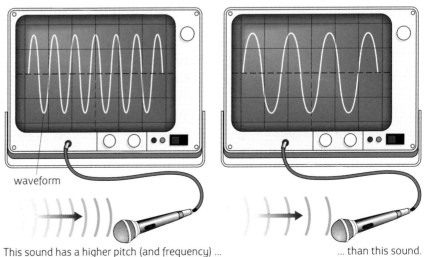

waveform

This sound has a higher pitch (and frequency) ...

... than this sound.

## Amplitude and loudness

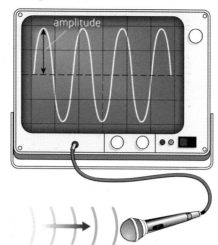
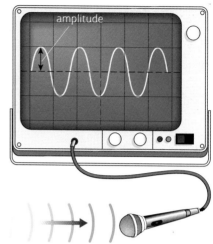

This sound is louder...                                                    ... than this sound.

Low **and** loud.

The sounds shown on the oscilloscope screens above have the same frequency. But one is *louder* than the other. The vibrations in the air are bigger and the **amplitude** of the waveform is greater. So:

The greater the amplitude, the louder the sound is.

## The wave equation

This equation applies to sound waves, just like other waves:

speed    =    frequency × wavelength

in m/s          in Hz          in m

The higher the frequency, the shorter the wavelength.

### Wave examples

The speed of sound in air is 330 m/s. From the equation on the right: sound waves of frequency 110 Hz have a wavelength of 3 m. Sound waves of frequency 330 Hz have a wavelength of 1 m.

## Questions

1. *Sound A: 400 Hz          Sound B: 200 Hz*

   Sounds A and B are played equally loudly. For someone listening to the two sounds, how would B compare with A?

2. A microphone picks up three different sounds, **X**, **Y**, and **Z**, one after another. On the right, you can see their waveforms on the screen of an oscilloscope.

   **a** Which sound has the greatest amplitude?

   **b** Which sound is the loudest?

   **c** Which sound has the highest frequency?

   **d** Which sound has the highest pitch?

3. In question **1**, which of the two sounds, A or B, has the longer wavelength?

4. Use the wave equation on this page to work out the wavelength of a sound whose frequency is 660 Hz. (Assume that the speed of sound in air is 330 m/s.)

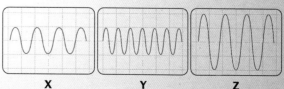

X          Y          Z

# Inside atoms

**This spread should help you to**
- explain what atoms, elements, and isotopes are
- explain what atomic number and mass number mean

Everything is made of atoms. Atoms are far too small to be seen with any ordinary microscope. However, by shooting tiny atomic particles through them, scientists have been able to develop **models** (descriptions) of their structure. Here is one simple model:

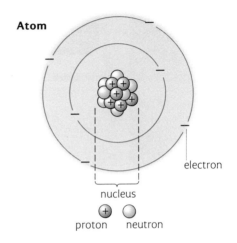

*A simple model of the atom. A real nucleus is far too small to be shown to its correct scale. If this atom were the size of a theatre, its nucleus would be smaller than a pea!*

- An atom has a central **nucleus** made up of **protons** and **neutrons**. Around this, **electrons** orbit at high speed, at set levels.
- Protons have a positive (+) electric charge. Electrons have an equal negative (–) charge. Normally, an atom has the same number of electrons as protons, so its total charge is zero.
- Protons and neutrons are much heavier than electrons, which add almost nothing to an atom's mass.

## Elements and atomic number

All materials are made from about 100 basic substances called **elements**. An atom is the smallest possible 'piece' of an element.

Each element has a different number of protons in its atoms: it has a different **atomic number** (or **proton number**). There are some examples on the left. The atomic number also tells you the number of electrons in the atom.

| Element | Chemical symbol | Atomic number (proton number) |
|---|---|---|
| hydrogen | H | 1 |
| helium | He | 2 |
| lithium | Li | 3 |
| beryllium | Be | 4 |
| boron | B | 5 |
| carbon | C | 6 |
| nitrogen | N | 7 |
| oxygen | O | 8 |
| radium | Ra | 88 |
| thorium | Th | 90 |
| uranium | U | 92 |
| plutonium | Pu | 94 |

## Isotopes and mass number

The atoms of any one element are not all exactly alike. Some may have more neutrons than others. These different versions of the element are called **isotopes**. Chemically, they behave in exactly the same way, although their atoms have different masses.

Most elements are a mixture of two or more isotopes. You can see some examples in the chart below.

The total number of protons and neutrons in the nucleus is called the **mass number** (or **nucleon number**).

Isotopes have the *same* atomic number but *different* mass numbers. For example:

The metal lithium (atomic number 3) is a mixture of two isotopes with mass numbers 6 and 7. Lithium-7 is the more common: over 93% of lithium atoms are of this type. On the left, you can see how to represent an atom of lithium-7 using a symbol and numbers.

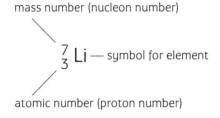

mass number (nucleon number)

$^{7}_{3}$Li — symbol for element

atomic number (proton number)

| Element | Isotopes | | e = electron (–) p = proton (+) n = neutron |
|---|---|---|---|
| **hydrogen** H | 1 e, 1 p, 0 n, hydrogen-1, $^{1}_{1}$H | >99% | |
| | 1 e, 1 p, 1 n, hydrogen-2, $^{2}_{1}$H | <1% | |
| **helium** He | 2 e, 2 p, 1 n, helium-3, $^{3}_{2}$He | <1% | |
| | 2 e, 2 p, 2 n, helium-4, $^{4}_{2}$He | >99% | |
| **lithium** Li | 3 e, 3 p, 3 n, lithium-6, $^{6}_{3}$Li | 7% | |
| | 3 e, 3 p, 4 n, lithium-7, $^{7}_{3}$Li | 93% | |

> means 'greater than', < means 'less than'.

## Questions

*For questions 4 and 5, you will need data from the table of elements on the opposite page.*

**1** An atom contains *electrons*, *protons*, and *neutrons*.

Which of these particles:

**a** are outside the nucleus?  **b** are uncharged?

**c** are much lighter than the others?

**2** An aluminium atom has an atomic number of 13 and a mass number of 27. How many of the following does it have?

**a** protons  **b** electrons  **c** neutrons

**3** Chlorine is a mixture of two isotopes, with mass numbers 35 and 37. What is the difference between the two atoms?

**4** In symbol form, nitrogen-14 can be written $^{14}_{7}$N.

How can each of the following be written?

**a** carbon-12  **b** oxygen-16  **c** radium-226

**5** Atom X has 6 electrons and a mass number of 12. Atom Y has 6 electrons and a mass number of 14. Atom Z has 8 neutrons and a mass number of 15. Identify the elements X, Y, and Z.

Nuclear radiation

Some materials contain atoms with unstable nuclei. In time, each nucleus breaks up, or rearranges itself. As it does so, it shoots out a tiny particle, a burst of wave energy, or both. The particles and waves 'radiate' from the nucleus, so they are called **nuclear radiation**. The materials they come from are **radioactive**.

Elements are a mixture of isotopes. In a 'radioactive material', it is really particular isotopes that are radioactive. The chart below gives some examples. Radioactive isotopes are called **radioisotopes**.

| Isotopes | | |
|---|---|---|
| *stable nuclei* | *unstable nuclei, radioactive* | *found in* |
| carbon-12 carbon-13 | carbon-14 | air, plants, animals |
| potassium-39 potassium-41 | potassium-40 | rocks, plants, sea water |
| | uranium-234 uranium-235 uranium-238 | rocks |

**Questions**

1 Name one radioisotope which occurs naturally in living things.

2 What are the three main types of nuclear radiation?

## Alpha, beta, and gamma radiation

There are three main types of nuclear radiation: **alpha particles**, **beta particles**, and **gamma rays**. The chart on the opposite page gives their main properties (features). Gamma rays are the most penetrating and alpha particles the least, as shown below:

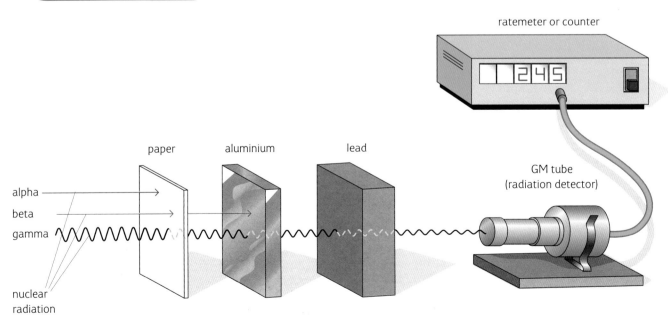

Alpha, beta, and gamma radiation can be detected using a **Geiger–Müller tube** (**GM tube** for short). The GM tube can be connected to the following:

- **A ratemeter** This gives a reading in counts per second. For example, if 50 alpha particles are detected by a GM tube every second, the ratemeter reads 50 counts per second.
- **An electronic counter** This counts the *total* number of particles (or bursts of gamma radiation) detected by the tube.
- **An amplifier and loudspeaker** The loudspeaker 'clicks' when each particle or burst of gamma radiation is detected.

## Ionizing radiation

Nuclear radiation can strip electrons from atoms in its path. As a result, the atoms are left electrically charged. Charged atoms are called **ions**, so nuclear radiation causes **ionization**. Ultraviolet and X-rays also cause ionization. Living cells are very sensitive to ionization. It can completely upset their life processes.

*Here, a GM tube is being used to check for traces of radioactive dust on the ground.*

| Nuclear radiation | Alpha particles | Beta particles | Gamma rays |
|---|---|---|---|
| | each particle is 2 protons + 2 neutrons | each particle is an electron (formed when the nucleus breaks up) | electromagnetic waves similar to X-rays |
| Electric charge | positive | negative | no charge |
| Ionizing effect | strong | weak | very weak |
| Penetrating effect | not very penetrating, stopped by thick sheet of paper, or skin | penetrating, but stopped by thick sheet of aluminium | highly penetrating, never completely stopped, though lead and very thick concrete reduce strength |

## Questions

**3** What is a GM tube used for?

**4** Nuclear radiation causes *ionization*. What does this mean?

**5** *alpha* *beta* *gamma*

Which of these three types of radiation:

**a** is a form of electromagnetic radiation?

**b** carries positive charge?

**c** carries negative charge?

**d** can penetrate a thick sheet of lead?

**e** is stopped by skin or thick paper?

**f** is similar to X-rays?

**g** is the most ionizing?

# Exposed to radiation

Nuclear power stations produce radioactive waste. The containers that carry the waste must be strong enough to withstand crashes like the one above. If any leaked out, it would be a health hazard.

## Radiation dangers

Because of its ionizing effect, nuclear radiation can damage or destroy living cells. It can stop vital organs in the body working properly, and cause cancer. The stronger the radiation, the greater the risk.

**Dangers from inside the body** Radioactive gas and dust are especially dangerous because they can be taken into the body with air, food, or drink. Once absorbed, they are difficult to remove, and their radiation can cause damage in cells deep in the body. Alpha radiation is the most harmful because it is the most highly ionizing.

**Dangers from outside the body** Normally, there is less risk from radioactive sources *outside* the body. Sources in nuclear power stations and laboratories are well shielded, and their radiation gets weaker as you move further away from them. Beta and gamma rays are the most dangerous because they can penetrate to internal organs. But alpha particles are stopped by the skin.

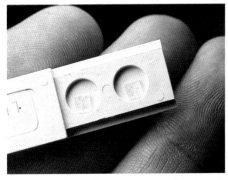

*This film badge detects the total amount of radiation the wearer has been exposed to.*

Workers in nuclear power stations have to wear a film badge like the one on the left. It reacts to nuclear radiation rather like the film in a camera reacts to light. Every month, the film is developed, to check that its wearer hasn't been exposed to too much radiation.

## Background radiation

We are exposed to a small amount of radiation all the time because of radioactive material in our surroundings. This is called **background radiation**. It mainly comes from natural sources such as soil, rocks, air, building materials, food and drink – and even space.

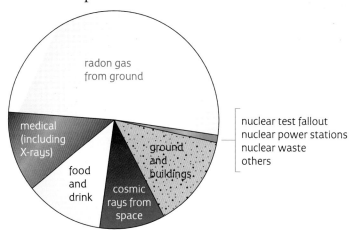

*Where background radiation comes from. (These proportions are averages. The actual proportions vary from one area to another).*

In some areas, over half of the background radiation comes from radioactive radon gas (radon-222) seeping out of rocks – especially some types of granite. In high-risk areas, houses may need extra ventilation to stop the gas collecting. Sometimes, a sealed floor is used to stop the gas entering in the first place.

When the radiation from a radioactive source is measured, the reading always *includes* any background radiation. To find the reading for the source alone, you must measure the background radiation and take that reading away from the total.

## Questions

**1** What is the biggest source of background radiation?

**2** Radon gas seeps out of rocks underground. Why is it important to stop radon collecting in houses?

**3 a** Which is the most dangerous type of radiation from radioactive materials absorbed by the body?

**b** Why is this radiation less dangerous outside the body?

**4** In the experiment on the right:

**a** What is the count rate due to background radiation?

**b** What is the count rate due to the source alone?

**c** If the source emits one type of radiation only, what type is it? (You may need information from the previous spread to answer this.)

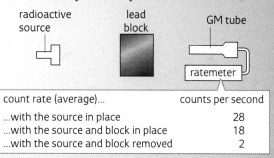

| count rate (average)... | counts per second |
|---|---|
| ...with the source in place | 28 |
| ...with the source and block in place | 18 |
| ...with the source and block removed | 2 |

# Radioactive decay

The break-up of unstable nuclei is called **radioactive decay**. It happens completely at random, and isn't affected by pressure, temperature, or chemical change. You can't tell which nucleus is going to break up next, or when. However, some types of nucleus are more unstable than others and decay at a faster rate.

## Activity

In a radioactive sample, the average number of nuclei breaking up per second is called the **activity**. Activity is measured in **becquerels** (Bq). For example:

Iodine-131 is a radioactive isotope of iodine. It decays by shooting out beta particles. If, in a sample of iodine-131, 40 nuclei are breaking up every second, then 40 beta particles are being shot out every second, and the activity of the sample is 40 Bq.

## Half-life

| Time in days | Activity in Bq |
|:---:|:---:|
| 0 | 40 |
| 8 | 20 |
| 16 | 10 |
| 24 | 5 |

*Every 8 days, the activity halves. Iodine-131 has a **half-life** of 8 days.*

The table and graph above show how the average activity of a sample of iodine-131 varies with time. To begin with, 40 nuclei are breaking up every second, so the activity is 40 Bq. But as time goes on, there are fewer and fewer unstable nuclei left to decay, so the activity gets less and less. After 8 days, the activity has fallen to half its original value. After another 8 days, the activity has halved again... and so on. Iodine-131 has a **half-life** of 8 days.

With experimental results, the points on the graph are irregular (they jump about) because radioactive decay is a random process. The curve above is really a 'line of best fit', as shown on the left.

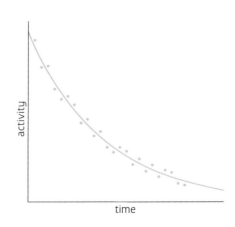

*The curve is really a 'line of best fit' between irregular points.*

| Radioactive isotope | Half-life |
|---|---|
| boron-12 | 0.02 seconds |
| radon-220 | 52 seconds |
| iodine-128 | 25 minutes |
| radon-222 | 3.8 days |
| strontium-90 | 28 years |
| radium-226 | 1602 years |
| carbon-14 | 5730 years |
| plutonium-239 | 24 400 years |
| uranium-235 | 710 million years |
| uranium-238 | 4500 million years |

To get a graph like the one on the opposite page, a Geiger–Müller (GM) tube is used to detect the radiation from the sample. The number of counts per second is proportional to the activity – but not equal to it, because not all the beta particles from the sample go into the detector.

The half-lives of some other radioactive isotopes are given in the table on the left.

The half-life of a radioactive isotope is the time taken for the activity of any sample to fall to half its original value.

## New atoms from old

When an atom shoots out an alpha or beta particle, the number of protons in its nucleus changes, so it becomes an atom of a completely different element. Here is an example:

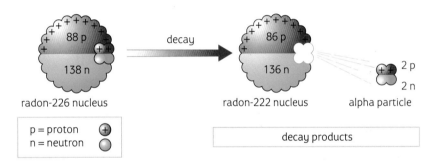

radon-226 nucleus

p = proton
n = neutron

decay

86 p
136 n

radon-222 nucleus

2 p
2 n
alpha particle

decay products

**Did you know?**

**Isotopes**

Most elements are a mixture of isotopes – different versions of the element, with the same number of protons in the nucleus of each atom, but different numbers of neutrons.

Above, a nucleus of radium-226 decays by shooting out an alpha particle. As a result, the nucleus loses 2 protons and 2 neutrons, so it changes into a nucleus of radon-222. This too is radioactive.

Radon-222 and the alpha particle are the **decay products**.

## Questions

*To answer questions 1 and 2, you will need information from the table of half-lives.*

1 If samples of strontium-90 and radium-226 both have the same activity today, which will have the lower activity in 10 years' time?

2 If the activity of a sample of iodine-128 is 800 Bq, what would you expect the activity to be after:

   **a** 25 minutes? **b** 50 minutes? **c** 100 minutes?

3 The graph on the right shows how the activity of a small radioactive sample varied with time.

   **a** Why are the points not on a smooth curve?

   **b** Estimate the half-life of the sample.

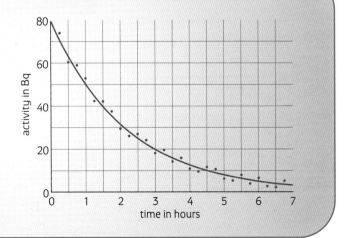

# Using radioactivity

**This spread should help you to**

- describe some of the uses of radioisotopes

**Did you know?**

**Nuclear essentials**

Elements exist in different versions, called isotopes. Some are radioactive: they are **radioisotopes**. Of the radiation they give off, gamma rays are very penetrating, beta particles less so, and alpha particles least of all. All three types of radiation damage or destroy living cells if absorbed.

Some radioisotopes exist naturally; others must be produced artificially in a nuclear reactor. Here are some of their uses.

## Using tracers

Radioisotopes can be detected in very small (and safe) quantities, so they can be used as **tracers** – their movements can be tracked. Here are two examples:

- Checking whether a patient's thyroid gland is taking in iodine properly. The patient drinks a liquid containing iodine-123, a gamma emitter. A detector measures the activity of the tracer to find out how quickly iodine becomes concentrated in the gland.
- Detecting leaks in underground pipes by adding a tracer to the fluid in the pipe.

For tests like these, artificial radioisotopes with short half-lives are used so that there is almost no radioactivity left after a few days.

## Radiotherapy

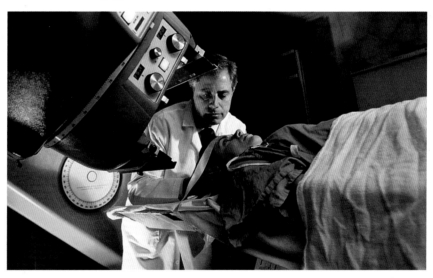

*A concentrated beam of gamma rays is pointed at one small area of this patient's body to kill the cancer cells in a tumour.*

Gamma rays can penetrate deep into the body and kill living cells. So a highly concentrated beam from a cobalt-60 source can be used to kill cancer cells. Treatment like this is called **radiotherapy**.

## Testing for cracks

Gamma rays are like X-rays, so they can be used to photograph metals to reveal cracks. A cobalt-60 gamma source is compact and does not need an electrical power source like an X-ray tube.

### Questions

**1 a** What are *radioisotopes*?

**b** Where are artificial radioisotopes produced?

**c** Give *two* medical uses of radioisotopes.

**2** Give *two* uses of gamma radiation.

## Thickness monitoring

Some material manufacturing processes need to produce a steady thickness. The diagram shows one way of doing this. The thickness of tyre cord is being adjusted:

*The moving band of tyre cord has a beta source on one side and a detector on the other. If the cord from the rollers becomes too thin, more beta radiation reaches the detector. This sends signals to the control unit, which adjusts the gap between the rollers.*

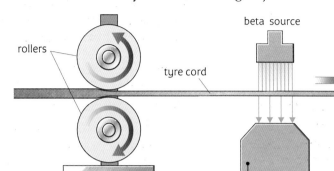
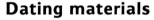

## Dating materials

*Human remains from a Danish peat bog. Carbon dating showed that this man died around 220–240 BC.*

As time goes on, any radioactivity in a material slowly dies away. This idea can be used to estimate its age. For example:

There is carbon in the atmosphere (in carbon dioxide) and in the bodies of living things. A small amount is radioactive carbon-14, which is continually being formed in the upper atmosphere. While plants and animals are alive, they absorb and give out carbon as they feed and breathe, so the proportion of carbon-14 in their bodies stays the same. But when they die, no more carbon is taken in and the proportion of carbon-14 reduces because of radioactive decay.

By measuring the activity of a sample, the age of the remains can be estimated. This is called **carbon dating**. It can be used to find the age of organic materials such as wood and cloth.

The age of some rocks can also be estimated by measuring the proportions of different isotopes in them.

## Questions

**3** In the thickness monitoring system shown above:

  **a** why is a beta source used, rather than an alpha or gamma source?

  **b** what is the effect on the detector if the thickness of the tyre cord increases?

**4** Doctors and scientists sometimes use radioactive tracers.

  **a** What is a radioactive tracer?

  **b** Describe one use of a radioactive tracer.

  **c** Why is it important to use radioactive tracers with short half-lives?

**5** Carbon-14 is a rare, radioactive isotope of carbon. Explain why scientists might be interested in measuring the amount of carbon-14 in the remains of an ancient plant or animal, or piece of wood or cloth.

# Models of the atom

From experiments carried out in the last century, scientists have been able to develop and improve their **models** (descriptions) of atoms and the particles in them.

## Thomson's 'plum pudding' model

At one time, scientists thought that atoms were the smallest bits of matter you could have. Then in 1897, J. J. Thomson discovered that atoms could give out tiny, charged particles which he called **electrons**. Electrons have a negative (–) charge; as atoms have no overall charge, this suggested that they must also contain positive (+) charge to balance the charge on the electrons.

Thomson suggested that an atom might be a sphere of positive charge with electrons dotted about inside it, rather like raisins in a pudding. People called this the '**plum pudding**' model.

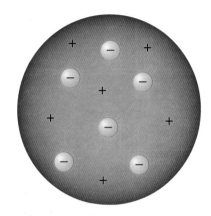

*Thomson's 'plum pudding' model of the atom.*

## Rutherford's nuclear model

In 1911, Ernest Rutherford got two of his assistants, Hans Geiger and Ernest Marsden, to do the experiment below. The results could not be explained by the plum pudding model.

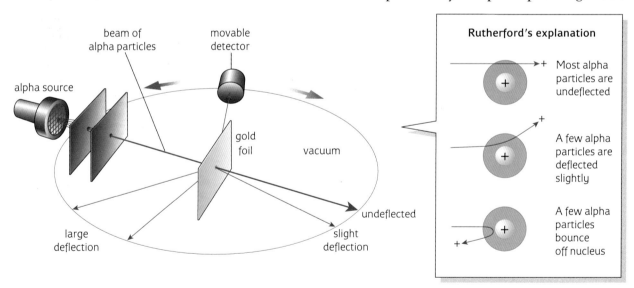

In the experiment, thin gold foil was bombarded with alpha particles, which are positively charged. Most passed straight through the gold atoms, but a few were repelled so strongly that they bounced back or were deflected through large angles. Rutherford concluded that the atom must be largely empty space, with its positive charge and most of its mass concentrated in a tiny **nucleus** at the centre. In his model, the much lighter electrons orbited the nucleus rather like the planets around the Sun.

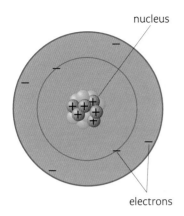

nucleus

electrons

*The Rutherford–Bohr model of the atom, with nuclear particles included. The particles don't really have colours. And if the nucleus were drawn to the right scale, it would be too small to see in this diagram.*

In 1913, Niels Bohr modified Rutherford's model by suggesting that electrons were only allowed to have certain orbits around the nucleus. He did this in order to explain some features of the light given out by atoms.

In 1919, Rutherford found that positively charged particles could be knocked out of the nucleus. These were **protons**. In 1932, James Chadwick found that the nucleus also contained uncharged particles, which he called **neutrons**.

## Modern models

Since Rutherford's time, scientists have had to develop new models to explain their discoveries. For example, electrons can behave like clouds of charge rather than points of charge. They can also behave like waves!

Today, scientists use a **wave mechanics** model of the atom. This is a mathemetical model, and can't really be shown in a picture. However, drawing a nucleus with electrons around it is still a useful way of representing an atom.

*Today, scientists use giant machines like this to smash atomic particles together and find out what they are made of.*

## Questions

1 What is the difference between Rutherford's nuclear model of the atom and Thomson's 'plum pudding' model?

2 On the right, alpha particles are being fired at a thin piece of gold foil. According to Rutherford's nuclear model of the atom:

   **a** why do most of the alpha particles go straight through the foil?

   **b** why are some alpha particles deflected at large angles?

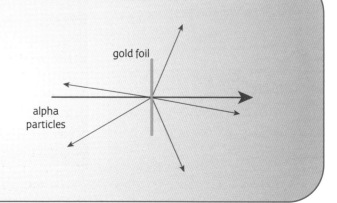

gold foil

alpha particles

# Ultrasound

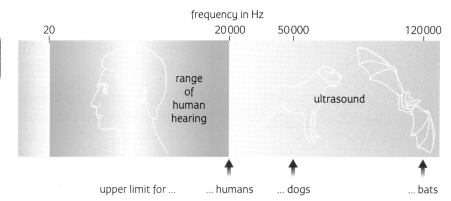

frequency in Hz

| 20 | 20 000 | 50 000 | 120 000 |

range of human hearing

ultrasound

upper limit for ... ... humans ... dogs ... bats

The human ear can detect sounds up to a frequency of about 20 000 Hz. Sounds above the range of human hearing are called **ultrasonic sounds**, or **ultrasound**. Here are some of the uses of ultrasound:

## Cleaning and breaking

Using ultrasound, delicate machinery can be cleaned without taking it to bits. The machinery is put in a tank of liquid. Then the vibrations of high-power ultrasound are used to shift the bits of dirt and grease.

In hospitals, concentrated beams of ultrasound can break up kidney stones and gall stones without patients needing surgery.

## Echo-sounding

Ships use **echo-sounders** to measure the depth of water beneath them. An echo-sounder sends pulses of ultrasound downwards towards the seabed, as shown on the left. Then it measures the time taken for each echo (reflected sound) to return. The longer the time, the deeper the water.

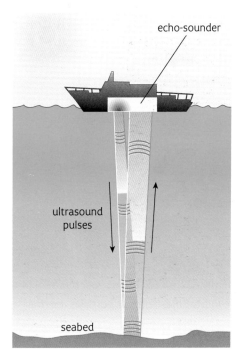

echo-sounder

ultrasound pulses

seabed

*A ship uses an echo-sounder to measure the depth of the water.*

## Questions

1 What is *ultrasound*?

2 What is an *echo-sounder* used for?

3 How does an echo-sounder work?

*This bat uses ultrasound to find insects and other things in front of it. It sends out ultrasound pulses and uses its specially shaped ears to pick up the reflections.*

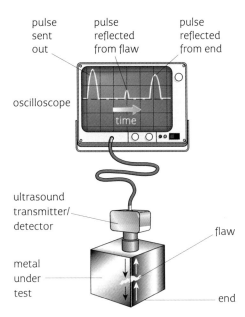

pulse sent out
pulse reflected from flaw
pulse reflected from end

oscilloscope

time

ultrasound transmitter/ detector

flaw

metal under test

end

*Using ultrasound to test a metal for flaws.*

## Metal testing

Flaws in metals can be detected using the echo-sounding idea. A pulse of ultrasound is sent through the metal, as on the left. If there is a flaw (tiny gap) in the metal, *two* pulses are reflected back to the detector – one from the flaw and the other from the far end of the metal. The pulses can be displayed using an oscilloscope.

## Scanning the womb

The pregnant mother below is having her womb scanned by ultrasound. A transmitter sends pulses of ultrasound into the mother's body. A detector picks up pulses reflected from the baby and different layers inside the body. The signals are processed by a computer, which puts an image on the screen.

'Seeing' inside the womb with ultrasound is much safer than using X-rays, because X-rays can cause cell damage in a growing baby.

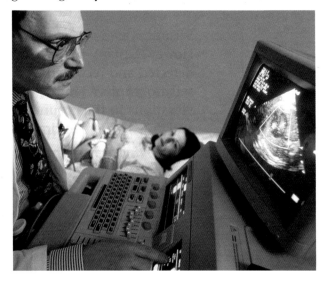

*An ultrasound scan of the womb. The doctor is moving an ultrasound transmitter/ detector over the mother's body. A computer uses the reflected pulses to produce an image.*

## Questions

**4** In hospitals, doctors can use ultrasound to 'see' into a pregnant mother's womb.

  **a** Why do doctors prefer to use ultrasound for this, rather than X-rays?

  **b** Give one other use of ultrasound in hospitals.

**5** Give *two* uses of ultrasound in industry.

**6** To answer this question, you will need the information on the right.

A boat is fitted with an echo-sounder which uses ultrasound with a frequency of 40 kHz.

  **a** What is the frequency of the ultrasound in Hz?

  **b** If an ultrasound pulse takes 0.1 seconds to travel from the boat to the seabed and back, how far does it travel?

  **c** How deep is the water under the boat?

| speed of sound in water = 1400 metres per second (m/s) |
|---|
| 1 kilohertz (kHz) = 1000 Hz |
| $\text{speed} = \dfrac{\text{distance travelled}}{\text{time taken}}$ |

# Radio waves from space

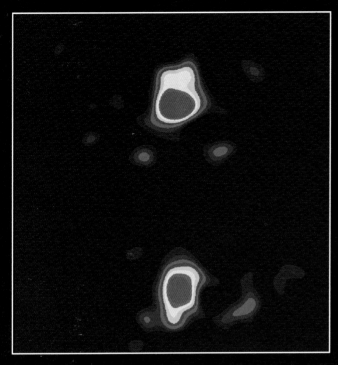

Stars, such as the Sun, give off light. But they give off other forms of radiation as well, including radio waves. **Radio telescopes** like those below pick up these waves. In space, radio signals can travel through clouds of dust that block light, so radio telescopes can 'see' stars that might be invisible through an ordinary telescope.

The image of distant stars on the left was created by a computer, using signals from a radio telescope. The colours are false.

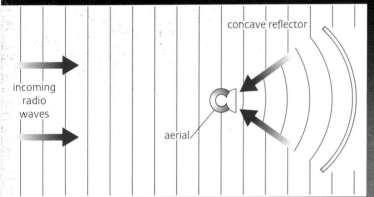

incoming radio waves

concave reflector

aerial

The main feature of most radio telescopes is a huge concave (dish-shaped) reflector. This focuses the radiation onto a tiny aerial. The dish needs to be large for two reasons. First, a large collecting area means that the faintest and most distant stars can be detected. Second, when incoming waves meet the dish, there is less diffraction. Any diffraction blurs the final image.

Building large dishes is difficult and expensive. An easier solution is to use an array of smaller dishes, as below, and combine the signals.

# Gamma fresh

These strawberries were picked three weeks before the photograph was taken.

So were the ones below, but these were put straight into a beam of gamma radiation. The radiation stopped the rotting process, so old strawberries look as fresh as the day they were picked.

Irradiating fruit could mean better quality, less waste, and lower prices. Although the radiation doesn't make the fruit radioactive, critics say that it may destroy vitamins and affect substances in the fruit. And when you next buy fresh strawberries, how fresh will they really be?

# Ultra-bright

The Sun's rays include some ultraviolet radiation. Although invisible to the human eye, it can be used to make things brighter!

**Fluorescent**, 'day-glo' paints contain chemicals which absorb the energy of invisible ultraviolet and give it off as visible light. It makes the paint look extra bright.

Some washing powders contain fluorescent dyes, called **brighteners**. They absorb ultraviolet and give off its energy as extra light, so your clothes look 'whiter than white'. Under ultraviolet disco lamps, some fabrics seem to glow!

In security-marking pens, the ink contains a fluorescent dye. The ink looks watery and can't normally be seen when dry. But a name or number written on your belongings shows up under a strong ultraviolet lamp.

## Talking points

By using the index, or other sources of information, see if you can find out which type of electromagnetic radiation:

- is similar to gamma rays and has the same effects.
- is used for satellite communication and mobile phone networks.
- comes from warm or hot objects.
- is sent along optical fibres.

# Fission power

Like most power stations, the nuclear power station on the right uses heat to make steam for the turbines which turn its generators. But the heat doesn't come from burning coal, oil, or gas. It comes from the nuclei of uranium atoms as they break up in a **nuclear reactor**. One tonne of nuclear fuel can deliver as much energy as 55 tonnes of coal.

In nuclear fuel, the 'magic ingredient' is a rare type of uranium called uranium-235. If a nucleus of uranium-235 is hit by a stray neutron, it splits, releasing energy and more neutrons. These may go on to split other nuclei...and so on, in a **chain reaction**. The splitting process is called **nuclear fission**.

In a reactor, pellets of nuclear fuel are in sealed cans in the reactor's core. As most neutrons tend to escape before hitting anything else, the core must carefully designed to make sure that the chain reaction keeps going. The reaction can be slowed down by lowering control rods to absorb neutrons.

In the reactor below, the heat from fission is carried to a boiler by water which circulates through the core.

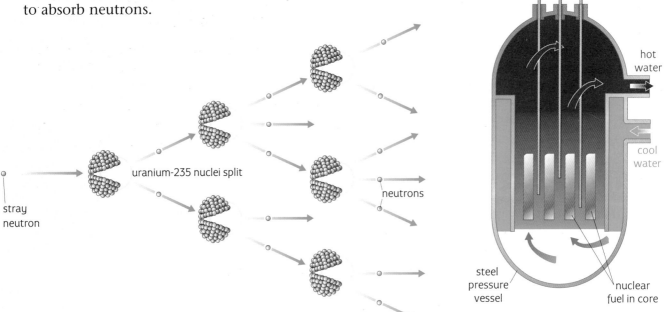

A pressurized-water reactor (PWR).

# Nuclear waste

When cans of nuclear fuel are 'spent' (exhausted), they must be removed from the reactor's core and replaced. They contain highly radioactive materials, including plutonium-239. Plutonium is used in nuclear weapons. It is also highly toxic. Breathed in as dust, the smallest amount can kill.

Spent fuel cans are taken to a reprocessing plant where unused fuel and plutonium are removed. The remaining waste is sealed off and stored with thick shielding around it.

Radioactive waste is extremely dangerous. Some isotopes have long half-lives and stay radioactive for thousands of years. No one really knows how to store them safely for such a long time. If they are buried, geologists must be sure that the rocks are stable and won't crack or move over that period.

# Fusion future?

The Sun is powered by **nuclear fusion**: energy is released when nuclei of hydrogen 'fuse' (join) together to form helium. For fusion to occur, hydrogen must be kept compressed at a very high temperature: for example 15 million °C in the Sun's core.

On Earth, no ordinary container can hold hydrogen at such a high temperature and keep it compressed. But the one above is no ordinary container. Scientists have developed it for fusion experiments. It uses a magnetic field to trap the super-hot hydrogen.

Practical fusion reactors are many years away. But they could bring huge benefits. Their fuel, hydrogen, is plentiful and can be extracted from sea water. Their main waste material, helium, isn't radioactive. And they have built-in safety: if the reactor fails, fusion stops.

## Talking points

⚠ Can you describe ways in which a nuclear power station is similar to a fuel-burning power station?

⚠ Can you describe ways in which a nuclear power station is different from a fuel-burning power station?

⚠ Why are 'spent' nuclear fuel cans such a problem?

⚠ When fusion reactors are developed, what advantages are they likely to have over today's nuclear reactors?

# Further topics

These further topics are included to satisfy the additional statutory requirements of the national curriculums for students in Northern Ireland and Wales.

# Turning and balancing

Forces can have a turning effect. In the diagram below, someone is using a spanner to turn a bolt. With a longer spanner, they could use the same force to produce an even greater turning effect.

The strength of a turning effect is called a **moment**. It can be calculated with this equation:

moment = force × distance from turning point

The distance is the *shortest* distance from the turning point to the line of the force. A turning point is also known as a **pivot**.

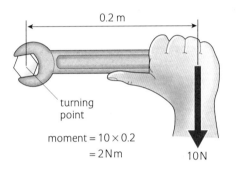

0.2 m

turning point

moment = 10 × 0.2
= 2 Nm

10 N

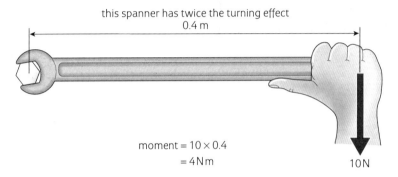

this spanner has twice the turning effect
0.4 m

moment = 10 × 0.4
= 4 Nm

10 N

## Moments in balance

Below, a plank has been balanced on a log. Weights have been put on the plank, and placed so that it still balances. One weight has a turning effect to the left, the other to the right. The two turning effects are equal, and cancel out. That is why the plank balances.

According to the **law of moments**, if something balances:

moment turning to the left  =  moment turning to the right

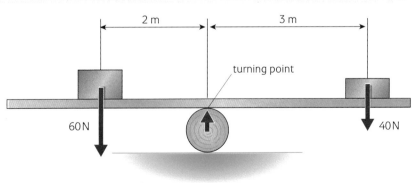

2 m          3 m

turning point

60 N          40 N

moment (to left) = 60 × 2 = 120 Nm —— these are equal —— moment (to right) = 40 × 3 = 120 Nm

**Questions**

1  How do you calculate the moment of a force?

2  If something is balanced, what does the law of moments tell you about it?

To balance on a beam, you have to keep your centre of mass over the beam. Otherwise your weight will have a turning effect and pull you over.

Suspend the card from one corner and draw a vertical line from it. Do the same using another corner. Then see where the two lines cross. This is the centre of mass.

## Centre of mass

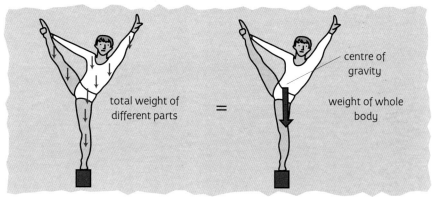

All the bits of your body have weight. Together, these tiny weights act like a single force pulling at just one point. This point is called your **centre of mass** (or **centre of gravity**). Simple shapes, such as a metre rule, often have a centre of mass exactly in the middle.

If you suspend a piece of card from some thread, it always hangs with its centre of mass in line with the thread. You can use this idea to find the centre of mass.

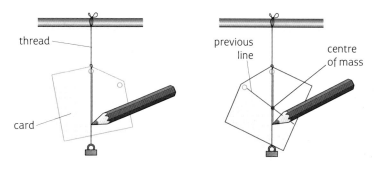

## Questions

**3** In diagram **A** on the right:

**a** which force, X or Y, has the greater turning effect on the nut? Explain your answer.

**b** how could the turning effect of force Y be increased?

**4** In diagram **B** on the right, the plank is balanced:

**a** What is the moment of the 100 N force about point O?

**b** What moment must the 400 N force have to balance this?

**c** What is the distance of the 400 N force from O?

**5** Where would you expect the centre of mass of a metre ruler to be? How would you check this by experiment?

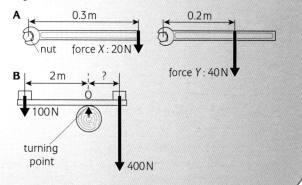

Pressure

*Skis reduce the pressure on the snow by increasing the area which must support your weight.*

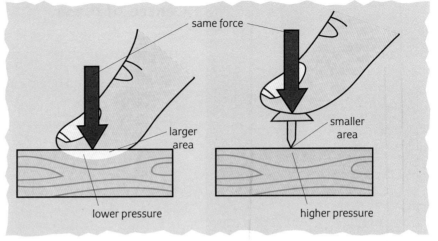

You can't push your thumb into wood. But you can push a drawing pin in using the same force, because the force is concentrated on a much smaller area. Scientifically speaking, the **pressure** is higher.

Pressure is measured in **newtons per square metre** (N/m$^2$), also called **pascals** (Pa). It can be calculated with this equation:

$$\text{pressure} = \frac{\text{force}}{\text{area}}$$

force in newtons (N)
area in square metres (m$^2$)
pressure in pascals (Pa)

For example, if a force of 1200 N pushes (at right-angles) on an area of 4 m$^2$: pressure $= \dfrac{1200}{4} = 300\,\text{N/m}^2 = 300\,\text{Pa}$.

### Liquid pressure

The deeper you go into a liquid, the greater the pressure becomes. This pressure pushes in all directions. It is the pressure from water which keeps a boat afloat. Water pressing on the hull produces an upward push called an **upthrust** which is strong enough to support the weight of the boat.

## Questions

1 Why is it easier to walk on soft sand if you have flat shoes rather than shoes with small heels?

2 If a force of 12 N presses (at right-angles) on an area of 4 m$^2$, what is the pressure?

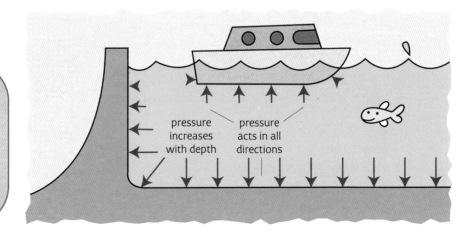

pressure increases with depth

pressure acts in all directions

## Hydraulic machines

These are machines in which liquids are used to transmit forces. Machines like this rely on two features of liquids:

- Liquids cannot be squashed. They are virtually incompressible.
- If a trapped liquid is put under pressure, the pressure is transmitted throughout the liquid.

The diagram below shows a simple hydraulic jack. When you press on the narrow piston, the pressure is transmitted by the oil to the wide piston. It produces an output force which is larger than the input force. In other words, it is a **force magnifier**.

Follow the sequence of circled numbers 1–4 on the diagram. They show you how to use the link between pressure, force, and area to calculate the output force.

*The shovel on this digger is moved hydraulically.*

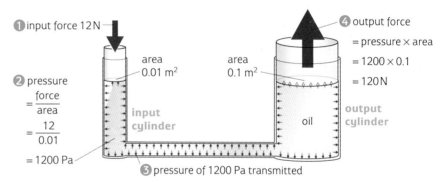

**1** input force 12 N

**2** pressure
$$= \frac{\text{force}}{\text{area}}$$
$$= \frac{12}{0.01}$$
$$= 1200 \text{ Pa}$$

area 0.01 m²   area 0.1 m²

**input cylinder**   oil   **output cylinder**

**3** pressure of 1200 Pa transmitted

**4** output force
= pressure × area
= 1200 × 0.1
= 120 N

Car brakes work hydraulically. When the brake pedal is pressed, a piston puts pressure on trapped brake fluid. The pressure is transmitted, by pipes, to the wheels. There, the pressure pushes on pistons which move the brake pads.

## Questions

**3** A rectangular block measures 4 m × 3 m × 2 m. It weighs 600 N and rests with one face on level ground. Draw a diagram to show the position of the block when the pressure under it is **a** as high as possible, **b** as low as possible.

Calculate the pressure in each case.

(Area of a rectangle = length × width)

**4** In the simple hydraulic system on the right:

**a** what is the pressure of the oil?

**b** what is the output force?

**c** if the diameter of the output cylinder were greater, how would this affect the output force?

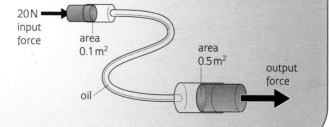

20 N input force   area 0.1 m²   area 0.5 m²   output force   oil

## FT3 · Stretching and compressing

### Objectives

**This spread should help you to**

- describe how wires stretch
- describe how the pressure of a gas depends on its volume

*The steel cables on this bridge mustn't exceed their elastic limit.*

### Stretching a wire

When bridge-builders use steel cables, they need to know how much they will stretch and what load they can safely carry.

The experiment below shows the effect of a stretching force on a long, thin, steel wire. As the force increases, so does the **extension** (the length by which the cable stretches).

A graph of *extension* against *stretching force* is straight up to point X. Within this straight section:

- Each extra 100 N (newtons) of force produces the same extra extension (1 mm in this case).
- If the force doubles, the extension doubles, and so on.

If a material produces a straight-line graph like this, scientists say that it obeys **Hooke's law**. Steel and other metals obey Hooke's law. So do steel springs. But rubber and many plastics do not. With these materials, the graph would be a curve, not a straight line.

Point E on the graph is called the **elastic limit**. Up to this point, the cable will return to its original length if the force is removed. Scientifically speaking, the material is **elastic**. Beyond E, the cable becomes permanently stretched. At Y, it breaks. If a material does *not* return to its original shape when the stretching force is removed, then it is **inelastic**.

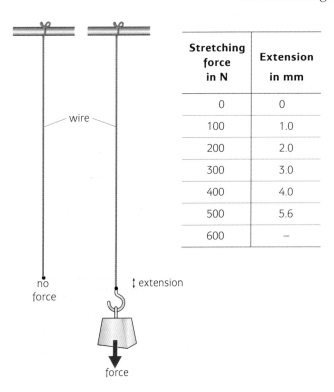

| Stretching force in N | Extension in mm |
|:---:|:---:|
| 0 | 0 |
| 100 | 1.0 |
| 200 | 2.0 |
| 300 | 3.0 |
| 400 | 4.0 |
| 500 | 5.6 |
| 600 | – |

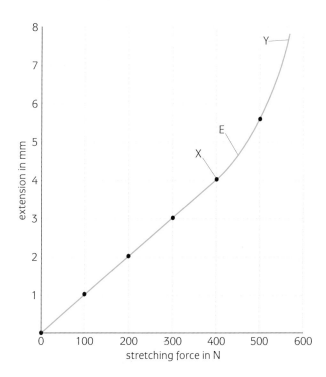

## Compressing a gas

If you squash a gas into a smaller volume, its pressure rises. The experiment below is designed to find out more about the link between pressure and volume. Some gas (air) is trapped in a cylinder. The gas is compressed by pushing in the piston, and the pressure and volume are measured at different stages.

Compressing the gas heats it up, which also affects the pressure. So the compression must be carried out very slowly so that the gas can lose heat and keep a steady temperature.

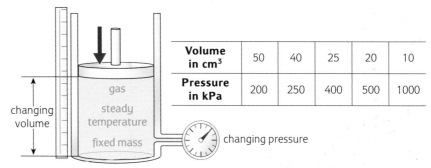

| Volume in cm³ | 50 | 40 | 25 | 20 | 10 |
|---|---|---|---|---|---|
| Pressure in kPa | 200 | 250 | 400 | 500 | 1000 |

The table gives some typical readings. They show that:

- If the volume is *halved*, the pressure is *doubled,* and so on.
- Pressure × volume keeps the same value (10 000 in this case).

These results are summed up by **Boyle's law**:

If a fixed mass of gas is kept at a steady temperature:

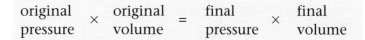

$$\text{original pressure} \times \text{original volume} = \text{final pressure} \times \text{final volume}$$

## Questions

*You will need graph paper for questions 2 and 3.*

**1** What is the difference between an *elastic* material and an *inelastic* one?

**2** When a spring was stretched, these readings were taken:

| Stretching force in N | 0 | 1 | 2 | 3 | 4 | 5 |
|---|---|---|---|---|---|---|
| Length in mm | 40 | 49 | 58 | 67 | 79 | 99 |

**a** Make a table showing *stretching force* and *extension*.

**b** Plot a graph of *extension* against *stretching force*.

**c** How can you tell if the spring obeys Hooke's law?

**d** If it obeys this law, up to what point does it do so?

**e** What force produces an extension of 21 mm?

**3** Look at the table above, giving volume and pressure readings for a trapped gas.

**a** Use the readings to plot a graph of *pressure* against *volume*.

**b** Describe what the graph shows.

**c** When the gas is at a pressure of 300 kPa, what is its volume?

**4** A balloon contains 6 m³ of helium. As it rises through the atmosphere, the pressure falls from 100 kPa to 50 kPa, but the temperature stays the same. What is the new volume of the balloon?

**1** A car driver drives from his home at a slow, steady speed. On reaching the motorway he accelerates rapidly and then travels at a high constant speed. Leaving the motorway he decelerates and comes to a halt at a junction.

  **a** Sketch a speed-time graph for the driver's journey.

  **b** Sketch a distance-time graph for the driver's journey.

  **c** Calculate the driver's average speed in km/h if he travels 40 km in 30 min.

**2** The diagram below shows a velocity-time graph for a free-fall parachutist.

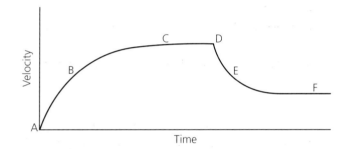

Assuming the acceleration due to gravity is 10 m/s$^2$

  **a** Why is the acceleration of the parachutist decreasing in part B of the graph?

  **b** Explain why the parachutist is travelling at his terminal velocity in part C of the graph.

  **c** What has happened at point D on the graph?

  **d** What is happening to the parachutist in part E of the graph?

  **e** What is happening to the parachutist in part F of the graph?

**3** An electric motor is a device for changing electrical energy into kinetic energy. Suggest a device which will carry out the following energy changes:

  **a** electrical energy to heat and light energy

  **b** chemical energy to electrical energy

  **c** light energy to electrical energy

  **d** sound energy to electrical energy

  **e** electrical energy to sound

  **f** chemical energy to heat and light

**4** **a** Explain the following sentences.

  Coal is a non-renewable source of energy.

  Wind is a renewable source of energy.

  **b** Name one other non-renewable source of energy.

  **c** Name one other renewable source of energy.

  **d** Give one advantage and one disadvantage of using the source of energy you have given as an answer for part c.

**5** The diagram below shows a simple series circuit containing a cell, a switch and a bulb. When the switch is closed a current of 0.2A flows through the bulb.

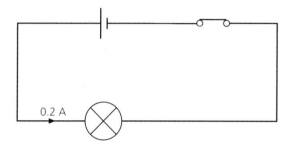

  **a** What current will flow from the cell if the second bulb is now connected in parallel with the first bulb?

**6** The diagram below shows a battery, ammeter and bulb connected in series. A voltmeter is connected in parallel with the bulb.

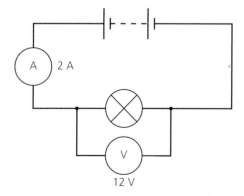

  **a** Calculate the power of the bulb.

  **b** How much energy is converted by the bulb in 10 s?

  **c** What energy change takes place inside the bulb?

**7** There are three commonly available fuses that can be used in a three pin mains plug. These are rated at 3 A, 5 A, and 13 A.

Which of these three fuses would be suitable for use with each of the following appliances? Electricity from the mains is supplied at 240 V.

**a** A bulb rated at 60 W.

**b** A TV set rated at 600 W

**c** A hair drier rated at 1.1 kW.

**d** A kettle rated at 2 kW.

**e** Explain what happens to a fuse if too much current passes through the circuit.

**8** The diagram below shows the inside of a three-pin plug.

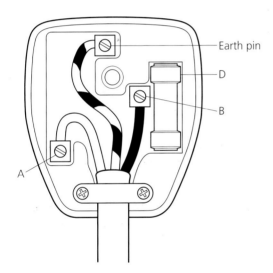

**a** What is the name of pin A?

**b** What is the name of pin B?

**c** What is the colour of the wire connected to the Earth pin?

**d** Explain why there is an Earth pin.

**e** What is D?

**9 a** If electrical energy costs 7p per kW h calculate the cost of the following:

    **i** a 3 kW fire turned on for 6 hours

    **ii** a 1.2 kW hair drier for 30 mins

    **iii** a 100 W bulb for 10 hours

**b** What is the National Grid?

**10** The diagram below shows two resistors connected in parallel.

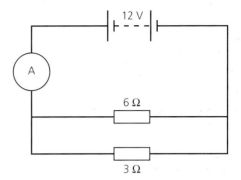

**a** What is A?

**b** Calculate the current flowing through the 6 Ω resistor.

**c** Calculate the current flowing through the 3 Ω resistor.

**d** What current flows through A?

**11** A student using the circuit shown below investigates the relationship between the current flowing through a resistor and the p.d. (voltage) across it.

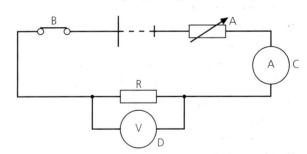

**a** What is A?

**b** What is B?

**c** What is C?

**d** What is D?

The student's results are shown in the table below.

| p.d./v | 0 | 2 | 4 | 6 | 8 | 10 | 12 |
|---|---|---|---|---|---|---|---|
| current/A | 0 | 0.25 | 0.50 | 0.80 | 1.00 | 1.25 | 1.50 |

**e** Plot a graph of p.d. against current.

**f** Which result appears to have been measured incorrectly?

**g** What is the resistance of the resistor R?

**12** A car headlamp is rated at 12 V 36 W.

  **a** What energy change takes place inside the bulb?

  **b** How rapidly does this energy change take place?

  **c** Calculate the current which flows through the bulb.

  **d** Calculate the resistance of the bulb.

**13** The graph below shows part of the journey of a bus driver. After travelling along the main road for several minutes he pulls into the bus station. Sometime later he drives out of the bus station and continues his journey.

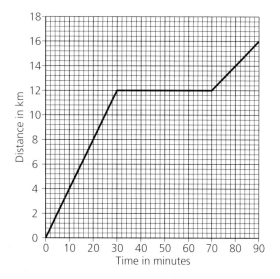

  **a** How far did the bus driver travel before pulling into the bus station?

  **b** How long did the bus driver stop in the bus station?

  **c** What was the average speed of the bus before pulling into the bus station?

  **d** Was the journey after the stop at a faster or slower speed? Explain your answer.

**14** The diagram below shows waves being produced in a ripple tank by a wave machine.

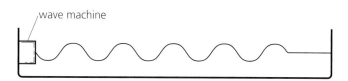

  **a** How many water waves are shown in the diagram?

  **b** If the above waves were produced in 2.5 s what is their frequency?

  **c** If the wavelength of the water waves is 5 cm calculate their speed.

**15** A crane lifts a load of 500 N through a height of 30 m in 20 s.

  **a** What kind of energy has the load gained after the lift has been completed?

  **b** Calculate the work done by the crane.

  **c** Suggest one reason why the crane will have done more work than the value you calculated in part **b**.

  **d** Calculate the power of the crane.

**16** The diagram below shows an electrical circuit.

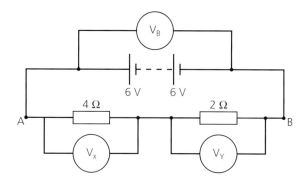

  **a** What is the voltage of the battery $V_B$?

  **b** What is the total resistance between points A and B?

  **c** What is the current flowing through the circuit?

  **d** What is the voltage ($V_X$) across the 4 Ω resistor?

  **e** What is the voltage ($V_Y$) across the 2 Ω resistor?

**17** The diagram below shows a bar magnet, and a coil of wire connected to a sensitive ammeter.

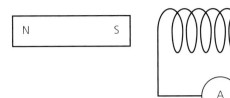

As the magnet was pushed slowly into the coil the ammeter pointer moved 10 divisions to the right.

What would you expect to happen

**a** If the magnet is pulled slowly out of the coil?

**b** The magnet is held stationary inside the coil?

**c** The magnet is turned around so that its north pole is nearer the coil. The magnet is then pushed quickly into the coil?

**d** Explain in your own words why the ammeter deflects.

**18** The diagram below shows the flow of heat from the inside of a house to the outside through a cavity wall.

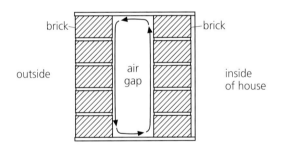

**a** Why will heat flow from the inside of a house to the outside?

**b** By what method is heat transferred through the bricks?

**c** By what method is heat transferred across the air gap?

**d** Suggest what could be done to reduce the rate at which heat flows across the air gap.

**19** Coal, oil and gas are fossil fuels.

**a** How is the energy contained in these fuels released?

**b** Explain briefly how fossil fuels are formed.

**c** Why are fossil fuels called non renewable sources of energy?

**d** Name one renewable fuel.

**e** Explain how the use of fossil fuels might lead to 'global warming'.

**20** The diagram below shows the flow of energy through a coal-burning power station.

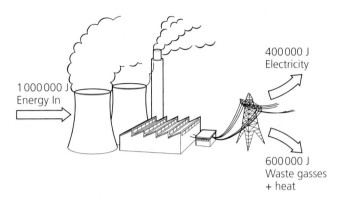

$$efficiency = \frac{useful\ energy\ output}{total\ energy\ input} \times 100\%$$

**a** Calculate the efficiency of the above power station.

**b** Explain how the energy released when the coal is burned is used to produce electricity.

**c** How is this electrical energy then sent to towns and cities many miles from the power station?

**21** The diagram below shows how light travels along an optical fibre.

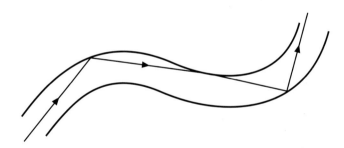

**a** Explain why the ray of light does not emerge from the sides of the optical fibre.

**b** Describe one use of an optical fibre.

**22** The diagram below shows the northern part of the Earth.

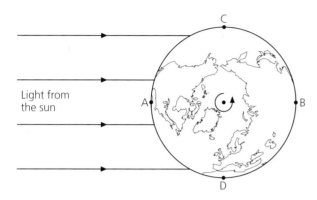

Light from the sun

Approximately what time of day is it

**a** at point A

**b** at point B

**c** at point C

**d** at point D on the Earth's surface.

**e** How long does it take the Earth to make one complete rotation around its axis?

**23** These objects are all part of the Universe.

planet   moon   satellite   constellation   Sun   comet   galaxy

**a** Which object is a very large collection of stars?

**b** Which two objects orbit the Sun?

**c** Which two objects could orbit a planet?

**d** Which object is a small collection of stars?

**e** Which is the largest object in our solar system?

**24** The diagram below shows what happens to the radiation from three different radioactive substances when different materials are put in front of them.

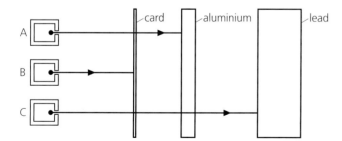

**a** Which type of radiation is being emitted by each of the three sources?

**b** Which of these three types of radiation are charged?

**c** Which of these three types of radiation is the strongest ionizer?

**d** Name one way in which all three types of radiation could be detected.

**25** The diagram below shows a toy car.

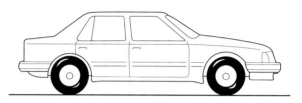

**a** Name three energy sources which could be placed in the car to make it move.

**b** What kind of energy does the car have when it is moving?

**c** Explain as fully as you can the phrase 'renewable source of energy'.

**26** The diagram below shows a tumble dryer.

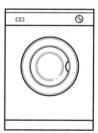

**a** Copy out the sentence below and fill in the missing words.

The tumble dryer converts _____ energy into _____ energy and _____ energy.

**b** The power of the dryer is 1.5kW.

Calculate the number of units of electricity it uses if it is turned on for 40 minutes.

**c** Calculate the cost of using the dryer for this time if the cost of 1 unit of electricity is 9p.

**27** This question is about the electromagnetic spectrum.

**a** Which statement about electromagnetic waves is correct?

A   They all have the same wavelength.

B   They all have the same frequency.

C   They all travel at the same speed in air.

**b** Name TWO types of electromagnetic wave which could be used to cook food.

**c** Name ONE type of electromagnetic wave used for communicating over large distances.

**d** Name ONE type of electromagnetic wave we use to see

**e** Describe the danger of ultraviolet radiation to our health.

**f** Suggest TWO ways in which people can reduce the health risk from ultraviolet radiation.

**g** Name ONE source of gamma rays.

**28** The diagram below shows a sledge sliding across some ice.

**a** As sledges slide across the ice, they slow down and eventually stop. Explain why this happens.

**b** Write down **two** effects the sliding sledges will have on the ice.

**29** Prisms can be used to alter the direction of a ray of light.

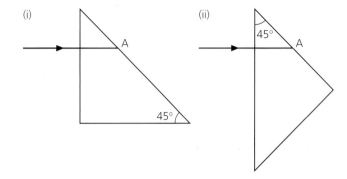

**a** Copy the diagrams below into your book and complete them showing accurately the paths the rays will take.

**b** What happens to each of the rays at point A inside the prisms?

**c** By how many degrees does each prism alter the directions of the rays of light?

**d** Name one use of a reflecting prism.

**1** The diagram below shows an electrical circuit containing a battery, two lamps and a switch.

Bulb A is identical to bulb B.

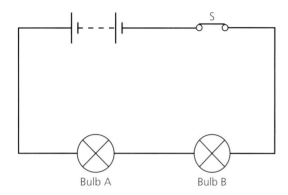

Bulb A          Bulb B

**a** In this circuit

A The current flowing through bulb A is larger than the current through bulb B.

B The current flowing through bulb B is larger than the current flowing through bulb A.

C The current flowing through bulb A is the same as the current flowing through bulb B.

D The current flowing through the battery is larger than the current flowing through bulb B.

**b** The total resistance of the two bulbs

A is less than the resistance of either bulb A or bulb B

B is equal to the resistance of bulb A minus the resistance of bulb B

C is equal to the resistance of bulb B minus the resistance of bulb C

D is equal to the resistance of bulb B plus the resistance of bulb A

**c** If the switch S is opened

A Bulb A will go out but bulb B will remain on.

B Bulb B will go out but bulb A will remain on.

C Bulb A and bulb B will remain on.

D The circuit will be incomplete.

**d** If the p.d. across bulb A is 6 V and the current flowing through it is 3 A, the resistance of the bulb is

A 18 Ω

B 0.5 Ω

C 2.0 Ω

D 3.0 Ω

**2** The diagram below shows three charged balloons. The middle balloon (B) has a positive charge.

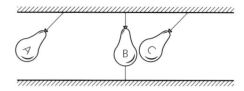

**a** Which of these statements is true about balloon B?

A Balloon B is uncharged.

B Balloon B has an excess of electrons.

C Balloon B has been given extra protons.

D Balloon B has lost some electrons.

**b** Which of these statements is true of balloon A?

A Balloon A is uncharged.

B Balloon A has the same type of charge as balloon C.

C Balloon A is positively charged.

D Balloon A is negatively charged.

**3** The diagram shows a household electricity meter at the beginning and end of a month.

| 1 | 5 | 1 | 0 | 3 |

start of month

| 1 | 5 | 6 | 7 | 8 |

end of month

**a** How many units of electricity were used during this month?

A 435

B 575

C 535

D 675

**b** During the next month 850 units of electricity were used. If the cost of one unit is 9p how much does this electricity cost?

A £86.50

B £76.50

C £72.50

D £85.00

**c** A 2 kW electric fire is turned on for 5 hours 30 minutes. How much electrical energy does the fire use?

A 9 Units

B 11 Units

C 12 Units

D 13 Units

**4** Choose one of the words below to complete these four sentences. Each word may be used once, more than once or not at all.

   A  convection

   B  conduction

   C  radiation

   D  insulation

   **a**  Heat travels from the Sun to the Earth by _____.

   **b**  Most of the heat from a radiator is transferred by _____.

   **c**  Heat travels along a metal rod by _____.

   **d**  Black objects are good absorbers of _____.

**5** The diagram below shows a car travelling at a constant speed along a flat road. Which of the following is true?

   A  There are no forces on the car.

   B  There are unbalanced forces acting vertically on the car.

   C  There are unbalanced forces acting horizontally on the car.

   D  The forces on the car are all balanced.

**6** Which of these has no effect on the stopping distance of a car?

   A  The kinetic energy of the car.

   B  The speed of car.

   C  The mass of the car.

   D  How far the driver can see.

**7** Which of these statements about electromagnetic waves is not true?

   A  Electromagnetic waves can travel through vacuum.

   B  Electromagnetic waves all travel at the speed of light.

   C  Electromagnetic waves are longitudinal waves.

   D  All electromagnetic waves can be reflected.

**8** Which of these diagrams shows what happens when a ray of light strikes a plane mirror at 90° to its surface?

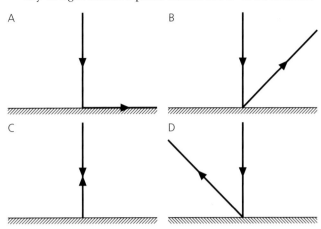

**9** Which of these ray diagrams correctly shows the path of a ray of light passing through a block of glass?

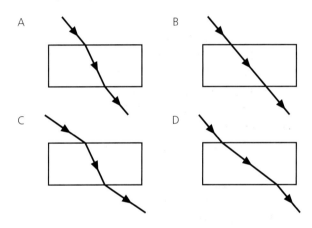

**10** Which of the following will not increase the rate of rotation of a motor?

   A  Increasing the current in the coil.

   B  Increasing the strength of the magnets.

   C  Increasing the resistance of the coil.

   D  Increasing the number of turns on the coil.

**11** Which of the following is not a kind of radiation given off during radioactive decay?

   A  Ultra violet radiation

   B  Alpha radiation

   C  Beta radiation

   D  Gamma radiation

# Revision and exam guidance

## How to revise

There is no one method of revising that works for everyone. It is therefore important to discover the approach that suits you best. These guidelines may help you.

**Give yourself plenty of time**  There are very few people who can revise everything 'the night before' and still do well in an examination the next day. You need to plan your revision to begin several weeks before the examinations start.

**Plan your revision timetable**  Draw up a revision timetable well before the examinations start. Once you have done this, follow it – don't be sidetracked. Stick your timetable somewhere prominent where you will keep seeing it – or better still put several around your home!

**Relax**  You will be working very hard revising. It is as important to give yourself some free time to relax as it is to work. So build some leisure time into your revision timetable.

**Ask others**  Friends, relatives, and teachers will be happy to help if you ask them. Don't just give up on something that is causing you a problem. And don't forget your parents too!

**Find a quiet corner**  Find the conditions in which you can revise most efficiently. Many people think they can revise in a noisy, busy atmosphere – most cannot! And don't try to revise in front of the television. Revision in a distracting environment is very inefficient.

**Use routemaps or checklists**  Use routemaps, checklists, or other listing devices to help you work your way logically through the material. When you have completed a topic, tick it off. Tick off topics you already feel confident about. That way you won't waste time revising unnecessarily.

**Make short notes and use colours**  As you read through your work or your textbooks, make brief notes of the key ideas and facts as you go along. But be sure to concentrate on understanding the ideas rather than just memorizing the facts. Use colours and highlighters to help you.

**Practise answering questions**  As you finish revising each topic, try answering some questions. At first you may need to refer to your notes or textbooks. As you gain confidence you will be able to attempt questions unaided, just as you will in the exam.

**Give yourself a break** When you are revising, work for perhaps an hour, then reward yourself with a short break of 10 to 15 minutes while you do something different. Look out the window, stretch your legs, have a soft or hot drink. But when your 10 or 15 minutes are up, get back to work!

## Success in examinations

Most people become a bit nervous about an important examination. If you have done most of your work consistently for two years and revised effectively, the following steps should help you to minimize anxiety and ensure that your examination results reflect all your hard work.

**Be prepared** Make sure you have everything you need ready the night before, including pens, pencils, ruler, and calculator. Check that you have anything else required well in advance.

**Read carefully** Before you start, spend a few minutes reading the paper all the way through. Make sure you know exactly what you have to do.

**Plan your time** Work out how much time you should spend on each question, based on how many marks it has. Allow yourself a few minutes at the end of the exam to check through your work.

**Answer the question!** When you are ready to start a question, read through it again carefully to make sure it really does say what you think it says. Follow the instructions to the letter: you will get marks for answering the question but not for giving other information about the subject.

**Present your work clearly** Write as clearly as you possibly can in the time available and think through what you are going to write before you begin writing. Draw diagrams clearly and simply, using single lines where appropriate. Label your diagrams and make sure the label lines point exactly to the relevant places. The examiner will be trying to award you marks – make it as easy for him or her to do so!

**Keep calm!!!** If you find a question you have no idea about, don't panic! Breathe slowly and deeply and have another look. It's likely that if you stay calm and think clearly, the question will start to make more sense, or at least you may be able to answer part of it. If not, then don't agonize about it – concentrate first on the questions you can answer.

$$\text{speed (m/s)} = \frac{\text{distance moved (m)}}{\text{time taken (s)}}$$

velocity (m/s) is speed in a particular direction

$$\text{acceleration (m/s}^2) = \frac{\text{change in velocity (m/s)}}{\text{time taken (s)}}$$

weight (N) = mass (kg) × gravitational field strength

(gravitational field strength = $g$ = 10 N/m$^2$ near Earth's surface)

work done (J) = force (N) × distance moved (m) in direction of force

work done (J) = energy transformed (J)

(energy transformed can also be called energy transferred)

gain in gravitational potential energy (J)
= weight (N) × gain in height (m)
= mass (kg) × $g$ × gain in height (m)

kinetic energy = $\frac{1}{2}$ × mass × speed$^2$
(J)                (kg)    (m/s)

$$\text{power (W)} = \frac{\text{energy transformed (J)}}{\text{time taken (s)}}$$

$$= \frac{\text{work done (J)}}{\text{time taken (s)}}$$

$$\text{efficiency} = \frac{\text{useful energy output (J)}}{\text{energy input(J)}}$$

$$= \frac{\text{useful work done (J)}}{\text{energy input (J)}}$$

$$= \frac{\text{useful power ouput (W)}}{\text{power input (W)}}$$

energy transformed = power × time
(J)                         (W)       (s)

energy transformed = power × time
(kW h)                    (kW)    (hours)

For waves:
speed (m/s) = frequency (Hz) × wavelength (m)

$$\text{resistance (}\Omega\text{)} = \frac{\text{voltage (V)}}{\text{current (A)}}$$

power (W) = voltage (V) × current (A)

$$\text{density (kg/m}^3) = \frac{\text{mass (kg)}}{\text{volume (m}^3)}$$

$$\text{pressure (Pa)} = \frac{\text{force (N)}}{\text{area m}^2}$$

moment of a force (N m)
= force (N) × perpendicular distance from pivot (m)

# Units and symbols

## Units and symbols

| Quantity | Unit | Symbol |
|---|---|---|
| mass | kilogram | kg |
| length | metre | m |
| time | second | s |
| force | newton | N |
| weight | newton | N |
| pressure | pascal | Pa |
| energy | joule | J |
| work | joule | J |
| power | watt | W |
| voltage | volt | V |
| current | ampere | A |
| resistance | ohm | Ω |
| charge | coulomb | C |
| temperature | kelvin | K |
| temperature | degree Celsius | °C |

## Bigger and smaller

To make units bigger or smaller, prefixes are put in front of them:

| | | |
|---|---|---|
| micro (μ) = 1 millionth | = | 0.000001 |
| milli (m) = 1 thousandth | = | 0.001 |
| kilo (k) = 1 thousand | = | 1000 |
| mega (M) = 1 million | = | 1000000 |

*For example*

| | | |
|---|---|---|
| 1 micrometre = 1 μm | = | 0.000001 m |
| 1 millisecond = 1 ms | = | 0.001 s |
| 1 kilometre = 1 km | = | 1000 m |
| 1 megatonne = 1 Mt | = | 1000000 t |

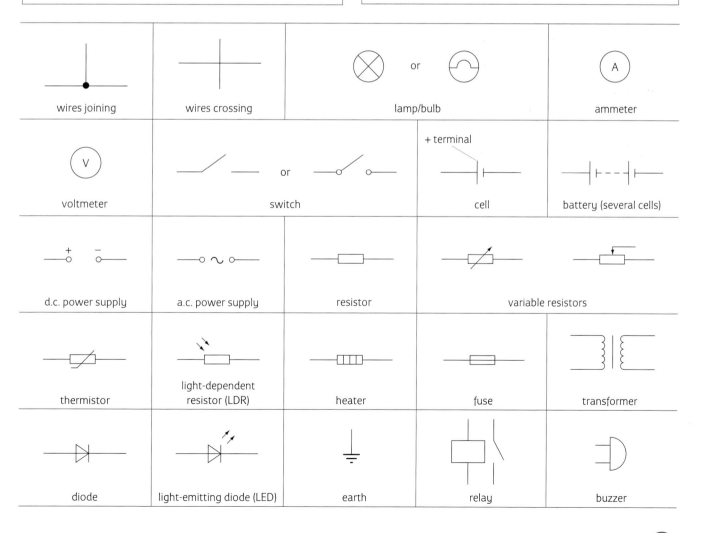

# Answers

Note: The answers are arranged in four sections
End of spread questions
End of module questions
Exam-style questions
Multiple choice questions

## End of spread questions

### Getting started S1
**1** kilogram (kg) **2** metre (m) **3** second (s)
**4** × 1000; × $\frac{1}{1000}$; × $\frac{1}{1\,000\,000}$
**5 a** 1600 g **b** 1.3 m
**6** 1st row – metre; 2nd row – Mass, kg;
3rd row – second, s
**7** gram, millimetre, milligram, tonne, millisecond, micrometre
**8 a** 1000 **b** 10 **c** 100 **d** 100 000 **e** 1 000 000
**9 a** 1000 mm **b** 1500 mm **c** 1534 mm
**d** 1.652 m
**10 a** 1000 g **b** 1.750 g **c** 26 000 kg **d** 6000 ms

### S2
**1 a** 2000 cm³ **b** 2000 ml
**2 a** 2700 kg **b** 27 000 kg
**3 a** 1 m³ of water **b** 1 kg of petrol
**4 a** X **b** Y **c** X
**5** X – steel, Y – aluminium

## Module 9.01
**1** joule (J) **2** petrol, food
**3 a** kinetic **b** 300 kJ **c** 6000 J

## 9.02
**2** changed into heat
**3 a** toaster **b** pole vaulter **c** sprinter
**4** energy changed into other forms
**5 a** kinetic energy → thermal energy (heat)
**b** chemical energy → elastic potential energy → electrical energy → sound

## 9.03
**1** metals **2** air trapped in them
**3 a** bottom must conduct, handle must insulate
**b** trapped air **c** water better conductor than air
**4 a** and **b** because of convection
**c** hot water rises by convection
**5** insulation in attic, walls; air in double glazing

## 9.04
**1 a** and **b** matt black **c** silvery
**2 a** absorb Sun's radiation **b** carry heat away
**c** silvery walls
**4 a** white reflects Sun's radiation
**b** black better absorber of radiation
**c** shiny surface poor emitter of radiation

## 9.05
**1 a** toaster **b** stereo **c** lamp **d** food mixer
**2** electric drill, vacuum cleaner, lawnmower
**3** food mixer – heat; stereo – heat; lamp – heat;
toaster – light
**4 a** watt **b** 2300 J **c** 23 000 J **d** 2.3 kW
**e** 12 kW

## 9.06
**1 a** watt, joule, kilowatt-hour b J, kWh
**2** 2 seconds
**3** switched on for less time
**4 a** 15 kWh **b** £1.50 (150p) **c** 0.1 kW
**d** 1.2 kWh **e** 12p
**5** Dan

## 9.07
**1 a** 40 N **b** 80 J **c** 160 J
**2 a** 6000 J **b** 300 J **c** 300 W
**d** lift load twice as fast

## 9.08
**1** useful energy output half of energy input
**2** transforms twice as much energy per second
**3 a** 0.4 (40%) **b** wasted as heat
**4** other 85% of energy becomes heat
**5** 200 W
**6 a** 3000 W **b** 3000 J **c** 0.75 (75%)

## 9.09
**1** 150 kJ **2** can't be used to produce motion
**3** engines can't use all input energy to produce motion
**4 a** less energy wasted as heat
**b** very low power input, so power wasted is very low
**5** filament bulb less efficient, so more energy wasted

## 9.10
**1** coal, oil, natural gas, nuclear fuel **2** nuclear

**3 a** boiler **b** turning turbines **c** turbines
**d** condense steam

**4 a** in turbines **b** heat **c** X 2000 MW, Y 500 MW
**e** X

## 9.11

**1** hydroelectric, tidal, wind farm

**2** global warming

**3** by water rushing from behind dam

**4** generator turned by wind turbine

**5 a** acid rain **b** fitting FGD units

**6 a** no carbon dioxide emitted **b** waste radioactive, leaked gas and dust spreads easily

## 9.12

**1** can't be replaced; oil, coal

**2** hydroelectric, wind farm

**3** Sun → plants → oil → petrol

**4** fuel made from plant or animal matter

**5** non-renewable, global warming

**6 a** Middle East **b** natural gas **c** North America, Europe

## 9.14

**1** to meet rapid increase in demand

**2 a** B **b** C

**3** wind farm, tidal power scheme

**4 a** to store energy **b** when demand for electricity is low **c** turns generators **d** uses spare capacity when demand is low, helps supply when demand is high

## Module 10.01

**1 a** current **b** conductor **c** insulator

**2 a** copper **b** PVC

**3 a** cell **b** generator

**4 a** torch, portable radio **b** any two mains appliances

**5 a** electric drill, food mixer **b** iron, toaster
**c** telephone, radio

## 10.02

**1** cell, complete circuit

**2 a** cell **b** switch **c** bulb

**3 a** ammeters **b** same **c** go out **d** go out
**e** zero **f** zero

**4** 2000 mA

## 10.03

**2** voltmeter **3** voltage

**4 a** battery **b** bulbs **c** 2 V **d** 3 V
**e** X 8 V, Y 4 V, Z 4 V

**5** 4 V

## 10.04

**1** ohm ($\Omega$) **2** resistance = voltage/current

**3 a** resistance can be varied **b** bulb brighter; less resistance in circuit

**4** more resistance **5** A 4 $\Omega$, B 1.5 $\Omega$, C 0.4 $\Omega$

## 10.05

**1 a** thermistor **b** diode

**2 a** 1 A **b** 3 A **c** 2 $\Omega$ **d** 4 $\Omega$

**3** 1st row **4** $\Omega$, 2nd row 1 A, 4 $\Omega$, 3rd row 0.5A, 4 $\Omega$

## 10.06

**2 a** A OFF, B ON **b** A OFF, B OFF

**3 a** 8 V **b** 2 A **c** 4 A **4 a** 2 V **b** 4 V

## 10.07

**1** 12 V **2** A 4 $\Omega$, B 15 V, C 1.5 A, D 0.5 $\Omega$

**3 a** 3 A **b** 1.5 A **c** 4.5 A

## 10.08

**1** north-seeking, south-seeking

**2 a** and **b** S-pole **3** using compass

**4 a** N-poles at top, S-poles at bottom
**b** apart, S-poles repel
**c** steel stays magnetized, iron doesn't

## 10.09

**1 a** higher current, more turns
**b** reverse current
**c** put steel rod in coil, pass current through coil

## 10.10

**1** loses magnetism when current through coil switched off

**2** higher current, more turns **3** reverse current

**4 a** smaller current through switch
**b** electromagnet closes contacts to complete output circuit

**5 a** break circuit if current too high b can be reset c break circuit at lower current

## 10.11

**1** **a** greater force  **b** force reversed

**2** **a** higher current, stronger magnet
**b** reverse current, reverse magnet

**3** every time current reverses, force reverses

**4** **a** stronger turning effect  **b** turning effect reversed

## 10.12

**1** **a** brushes  **b** commutator

**2** **a** currents are in opposite directions
**b** higher current, stronger magnet
**b** reverse current, reverse magnet

**3** will work on AC

## 10.13

**1** plus (+), minus (–)  **2** taken from atoms in hair

**3** **a** attract  **b** repel  **c** attract

**4** **a** electrons taken from atoms in sleeve
**b** attracted charges closer than repelled ones

## 10.14

**1** **a** sparks when aircraft refuelled  **b** earthing

**2** **a** pushed down  **b** inkjet printer  **c** pulled up

**3** charged atoms (or groups of atoms)

**4** contains ions

## 10.15

**1** 230 V  **6 a** live  **b** earth  **c** live  **d** neutral

**7** **a** 13 A **b** 3 A **c** fault may not blow fuse

**8** **a** wire to bulb live even when switch is off
**2** alternating current **3** battery gives one-way current
(DC) **4** breaks circuit if current too high **5** stops
casing ever becoming live

## 10.16

**1** watt (W)  **2** 1600 W

**3** A (drill) 460 W; B (toaster) 690 W; C (stereo player)
92 W

**4** **a** A 0.46 kW, B 1.15 kW, C 0.92 kW, D 0.023 kW
**b** A 2A, B 5A, C 4A, D 0.1A **c** A 3A, B 13A, C 13A,
D 3A

## 10.17

**1** full voltage across each, independently switched

**2** fuses (or circuit breakers)

**3** **a** breaks circuit if current is too high
**b** can be reset

**5** AC backwards and forwards, DC one way

**6** current goes backwards and fowards 50 times a
second

## 10.18

**1** **a** current reversed  **b** no current

**2** **a** and **b** higher current  **c** no current

**3** **a** higher current  **b** current reversed
**c** higher current

## 10.19

**1** generate AC  **2** higher voltage (and current)

**3** **a** alternating current, direct current  **b** AC  **c** AC

**4** **a** increase AC voltage  **b** decrease AC voltage

**5** **a** connect rotating coil to outside circuit
**b** higher voltage (and current), higher frequency AC
**c** fixed coil, rotating magnet
**d** to change AC to DC

## 10.20

**1** **a** generation  **b** transmission

**2** **a** national supply network
**b** high demand can be met by power stations
outside area

**3** stepping voltage up or down

**4** to reduce current in cables

**5** stepping down voltage, distributing power

**6** transformers only work with AC

**7** in area of outstanding natural beauty

## 11.01

**1** 5 m/s  **2** velocity has direction

**3** speed changes by 4 m/s every second  **4** 12 m/s

**5** 4 s  **6** from 4 s to 9 s  **7** 9 m/s

**8** 3 m/s$^2$  **9** 9 s  **10** 2 m/s

## 11.02

**1** **a** D  **b** B  **c** A

## 11.03

**1** **a** accelerating  **b** steady speed
**c** decelerating (retarding)  **d** 30 m/s  **e** 25 s
**f** 30 m/s  **g** 3 m/s$^2$

**2** **a** stopped•  **b** AB  **c** BC  **d** 40 m, 10 s  **e** 4 m/s

## 11.04

**1** kilogram, newton  **2** **a** kg  **b** N  **c** N

**3** tension, weight, air resistance  **4** 20 N, 40 N, 5 N

## 11.05

**1** wheel bearings   **2** tyre, to stop skidding
**3** **a** tyre, brake pad   **b** shaft
   **c** roller bearings, grease
   **d** prevent wear and overheating
**4** streamlined wheels, frame, helmet
**5** **a** streamlining, less speed
   **b** less fuel used, less noise

## 11.06

**1** C and D
**2** **a** terminal speed   **b** air resistance   **c** equal
   **d** reduced, bigger 'chute means less speed for same
   air resistance

## 11.07

**1** **b** 6 N   **c** downwards
**2** **a** right   **b** gain speed   **c** less acceleration
   **d** more acceleration
**3** **a** left   **b** lose speed; resultant opposes motion
   **c** steady speed

## 11.08

**2** driver tired, affected by alcohol
**3** airbags, seat belts, crumple zone
**4** B, C, D   **5** **a** 15 m   **b** 18 m   **6** 50 m

## 11.09

**1** **b** 500 N   **2** equal but opposite force on gun
**3** force has almost no effect on massive Earth

## 11.10

**1** joule (J)   **2** 80 J   **3** 160 J   **4** joule (J)
**5** petrol, food   **6** **a** 50 J   **b** kinetic
**7** **a** elastic potential energy
   **b** changed into kinetic energy   **c** heat

## 11.11

**1** 5 000 000 J   **2** changed into heat   **4** **a** 8 J   **b** 32 J
**5** four times the KE to lose, so much greater braking
distance

## 11.12

**1** 1 day 2 1 year 3 a night b night c daytime 4 reflects
sunlight 5 planet appears to move relative to stars

## 11.13

**1** and **2** Mercury, Venus, Mars, Pluto   **3** Mercury

**4** **a** Mars, Jupiter, Saturn, Uranus, Neptune, Pluto
   **b** further from Sun
**5** **a** gravity   **b** Venus   **c** Earth   **d** reflects sunlight
   **d** hotter than Mercury, but further from Sun

## 11.14

**1** Venus   **2** pieces of rock and ice
**3** elliptical orbit takes it further out
**4** no solid surface
**5** meteor is flash of light, meteorite reaches ground
**6** **a** X   **b** X   **c** Z   **d** dust and gas stream off
   **e** reflects sunlight

## 11.15

**1** **a** travels over whole of Earth's surface
   **b** to keep speed   **c** communications, navigation,
research
**2** **a** go out into space   **b** fall back to Earth
**3** geostationary orbit, so satellite orbits at same rate as
Earth turns
**4** **a** A   **b** B

## 11.16

**1** and **2** hydrogen
**3** **a** star system   **b** our galaxy   **c** all the galaxies,
everything   **d** distance travelled by light in 1 year
**4** no; at different distances from Earth
**5** **a** 300 000 km   **b** 100 billion   **c** 100 000 light years
   **d** 100   **e** 8 minutes   **f** 4 light years
   **g** 9 million million km   **h** 36 million million km

## 11.17

**1** **a** huge cloud of gas and dust   **b** gravity
   **c** 4500 million years   **d** planets and moons
**2** **a** core   **b** hydrogen   **c** 6000 million years
**3** **a** huge red star   **b** core will become white dwarf
**4** **a** gigantic explosion of massive star
   **b** neutron star

## 12.01

**1** **a** longitudinal - backwards-forwards vibrations,
transverse - side-to-side vibrations   **b** transverse
**2** 1st row 32 m/s; 2nd row 32 m/s, 2 m; 3rd row 32
m/s, 32 Hz
**3** **a** B   **b** B   **c** A   **4** **a** 20 mm   **b** 12 mm

## 12.02

**1** **a** reflection   **b** refraction   **c** and **d** diffraction

**2** **a** reflected  **b** refracted  **c** diffracted
**d** diffracted less

## 12.03

**1** Sun, bulb   **2** paper, table
**3** **a** aluminium, snow,  **b** coal  **c** glass, water
**4** sunlight reaches Earth
**5** solar cells produce electricity
**6** shadows, we can't see round corners
**7** **a** 300 000 km/s  **b** more than 1 s

## 12.04

**1** **a** angle of incidence  **b** 60°
**2** **a** diffraction through net curtain
**b** holes in net very small, so wavelength must be very small for diffraction to occur

## 12.05

**1** refraction   **2** and **5** because of refraction
**3** **b** reflected back in same direction
**4** **a** spectrum b violet c red

## 12.06

**2** because of total internal reflection
**3** **a** carrying telephone signals, endoscope
**b** rear reflector
**4** for internal reflection above this angle, there is no refracted ray

## 12.07

**1** same speed, travel through empty space
**2** **a** light  **b** X-rays, gamma rays  **c** radio waves
**d** microwaves  **e** infrared  **f** light
**g** infrared, microwaves  **h** ultraviolet
**i** X-rays, gamma rays  **j** infrared  **k** radio waves, microwaves, light, infrared  **l** ultraviolet

## 12.08

**1** analogue varies continuously, digital pulses represent numbers
**2** make signals larger
**3** **a** pulses of light or infrared
**b** better quality, can carry more lots of information
**c** carry more signals, less power loss
**d** long waves diffract more than VHF
**5** **a** frequency modulation, amplitude modulation
**6** **a** 2 000 000  **b** 2 000 000 Hz  **c** 2000 kHz

## 12.09

**1** wavelength   **2** longitudinal, not transverse
**3** **a** vibrations **b** compressions
**4** **a** people can hear in air
**b** people can hear underwater
**c** sounds travel through walls
**4** can't hear bell in jar when air removed
**5** **a** no material to vibrate **b** sound diffracted
**6** oscilloscope shows graph, not waves

## 12.10

**1** sound much slower than light   **2** refraction
**3** jet plane  **4** 320 m  **5** **a** warm air **b** solid
**6** **a** 660 m  **b** 2 s

## 12.11

**1** A higher pitch than B  **2** **a** Z  **b** Z  **c** Y  **d** Y
**3** B  **4** 0.5 m

## 12.12

**1** **a** electrons  **b** neutrons  **c** electrons
**2** **a** and **b** 13  **c** 14
**3** different number of neutrons in nucleus
**4** **a** $^{12}_{6}$C  **b** $^{16}_{8}$O  **c** $^{226}_{88}$Ra
**5** X carbon, Y carbon, Z nitrogen

## 12.13

**1** carbon-14  **2** alpha, beta, gamma
**3** detecting alpha, beta, gamma
**4** creates ions (makes atoms gain or lose electrons)
**5** **a** gamma  **b** alpha  **c** beta  **d** gamma  **e** alpha
**f** gamma  **g** alpha

## 12.14

**1** radon gas from ground   **2** radon is radioactive
**3** **a** alpha  **b** can't penetrate skin
**4** **a** 2 counts per second  **b** 26 counts per second
**c** gamma

## 12.15

**1** strontium-90
**2** **a** 400 Bq  **b** 200 Bq  **c** 50 Bq
**3** **a** decay happens at random  **b** 1.5 hours

## 12.16

**1** **a** radioactive isotopes  **b** in nuclear reactors
**c** tracers, radiotherapy

**2** radiotherapy, testing metals for cracks

**3 a** alpha completely stopped, gamma not stopped at all **b** less beta detected

**4 a** small amount of radioactive material that can be tracked **b** checking thyroid function c almost no radiation left after a few days

**5** remains can be dated

## 12.17

**1** Rutherford's model has nucleus

**2 a** atoms are mostly empty space **b** some alpha particles bounce off nucleus

## 12.18

**1** sound with higher frequency than human ear can hear

**2** measuring depth of water

**4 a** safer for baby and mother **b** breaking up kidney stones

**5** cleaning, testing for flaws in metals

**6 a** 40 000 Hz **b** 140 m **c** 70 m

## 12.19

**1** earthquakes **2** seismograph

**3 a** Z **b** X **c** Y **d** Y **e** Z **f** Z **g** X

## Further topics

## X.01

**3 a** Y; force × distance greater **b** move Y further from nut

**4 a** 200 N m **b** 200 N m **c** 0.5 m

**5** in the middle

## X.02

**1** larger area, so less pressure

**2** 3 Pa

**3 a** 100 Pa **b** 50 Pa

**4 a** 200 Pa **b** 100 N **c** greater

## X.03

**1** elastic material returns to original shape after stretching force removed

**2 c** straight line **d** up to 3 N **e** 2.3 N

**3 b** pressure rises as volume decreased **c** 33 cm$^3$

**4** 12 m$^3$

## End of module questions

## Getting Started

**1** metre m, kilogram kg, time second, current A, celsius or kelvin °C or K, m$^2$, volume, force N.

**2 a** 1000 **b** 1000 **c** 1 000 000 **d** 4 000 000 **e** 500 000

**3 a** 3 m **b** 0.5 kg **c** 1.5 km **d** 0.25 s **e** 500 ms **f** 750 m **g** 2500 **h** 800 mm

**4** 24 cm$^3$, 4 cm, 10 cm, 5 cm

**5 a** 8 g/cm$^3$ **b** 9 g/cm$^3$ **c** 19 g/cm$^3$

**6 a** 10.8 g **b** 16.0 g **c** 200 g

**7 a** 5 cm$^3$ **b** 2 cm$^3$ **c** 9 cm$^3$

## Module 9

**1 a** C **b** B **c** D **d** A

**2 a** 60 000 J **b** 200 W **c** friction, noise

**3 a** 500 N **b** 10 000 J **c** electrical to gravitational potential **d** 1000 W or 1 kW **e** 20 000 J **f** friction, weight of bucket **g** lighter bucket, lubrication

**4 a i** non polluting **ii** intermittent energy **iii** find new sources, reduce oil usage

**5 a** kinetic energy **b** friction, heat

**6 a** can be replaced **b** rainwater **c** non polluting **d** flooding

**7 a** 40 000 **b i** 1 MJ **ii** 2 MJ all potential energy is converted to kinetic energy **c** 1.2 MJ **d** less demand

**8 a i** chemical **ii** kinetic **iii** gravitational potential **b** heat

**9 a** sunlight **b i** heat **ii** 80%

**10 a** network of wires carry electrical energy **b i** oil **ii** find new sources, reduce oil usage

**11 a i** coal, gas **ii** coal **iii** gas **iv** never used up **b i** intermittent **ii** unsightly

**12 a** good absorber **b** prevent heat loss **c** convection current **d** more sunlight **e** 2 kW **f** 5 m$^2$ **g** non polluting, intermittent

**14 a** 'water jacket' fibreglass/foam **b** heats whole tank **c i** 1000 **ii** 3000 J **iii** 1 200 000

**15** double glazing, loft insulation, cavity wall insulation, carpets and underlay, draft excluders

**16 a & b** Convection **c** Condensation **d** Convection

**17 i** 0.2 Wh **ii** 2.4 p

**18 a** 0.1 kW, 0.02 kW **b** 20 kWh **c** 100 kWh **d** £8 **e** heat

# Answers

## Module 10

**1 a** Yes, No, No, Yes, Yes  **b** conductor, insulator

**4 a** C  **b** B

**5 a** 6 Ω  **b** 0.5 A

**6 i** parallel  **ii** 4 A  **iii** 2 A  **iv** no effect

**7 i** series  **ii** 3 V  **iii** goes out

**8 a** 0.3 A, 0.9 A  **b** 6 W

**9 a** ammeter  **b** variable resistor  **c** voltmeter  **e** 0.79 A  **f** 8 Ω  **g** increases

**10 i a** all out  **b** just one out  **ii a** Family B  **b** 40 V 240 V  **c** 0.25 A 0.33 A  **d** No

**11 a** 2 A  **b** 12 W

**12 i** neutral blue, yellow/green, live brown  **ii** earth – safety  **iii** earth wire

**13** cable grip, incorrect pin for brown, loose earth wire

**14 a i** $S_1$  **ii** $S_1$ and $S_2$  **b** 8.5 A  **c** 13 A  **d** Y  **e** safety  **f** blue  **g** brown  **h ii** double insulation

**15 i** electrical energy to heat and light energy  **ii** 2 kW  **iii** casing  **iv** live wire  **v** 8.3 A  **vi** 13 A  **vii** too large a current  **viii** turn it off

**17 a** nails fall  **b** do not fall  **c** more current or turns  **d** electric bell, relay switch

**20 a** A to B  **b** moves to the right  **c** moves to the left

**21 a i** stronger magnet  **ii** more loops of wire  **iii** faster rotation

**22 a** generators, coal, oil, gas. Chemical energy → electrical energy  **b** safety  **c** voltage decrease, step down transformer  **d** change voltage using transformers

**23 a** stepdown

## Module 11

**1 a** acceleration, constant speed, slowing down, topped, acceleration, court speed

**2 a** Jane  **b** Emma  **c** 5 s  **d** 7 m/s

**3 a** reaction time, weather

**4 a** between feet and ice, between ice and bobsleigh  **b** streamline themselves  **c** stopping

**5 a** high  **b** high  **c** high  **d** low  **e** high  **f** low

**6 i** gravity; increases  **i** Newtons  **ii** gravitational potential; kinetic  **b** 2000 J or 2 kJ

**7 a** lead ball  **b** air resistance for braking

**8 a** 10 km/h/s  **b** 4 km/h/s, –4 km/h/s  **c** 10 m/s²

**9 a** 10  **c** 3 s  **d i** gravity  **ii** air resistance  **iii** downword  **iv** equal  **e** lower terminal velocity

**10 a** star  **b** satellite  **c** constellation  **d** galaxy

**11 a** receiving sunlight  **b** not receiving sunlight  **c** 1 day  **d** moon  **e** gravitational forces  **f** larger

**12 a** suns/stars  **b** moon  **c i** moving across stars  **ii** object orbiting  **d i** planet  **ii** weather satellite

**13 a** B  **b** B  **c** A  **d** above same place on Earth  **e** constant contact

**14 a** 12

**15 a** Jupiter  **b** Pluto  **c** Mercury  **d** Jupiter  **e** 0.2 years  **f** hotter closer to Sun

**16 a** Venus  **b** Jupiter  **c** Smaller gravitational force from Sun  **d** Between Mars and Jupiter  **e** 6 or 7 years  **f** ellipse

**17 a** Ice  **b** elliptical  **c** furthest from Sun, smallest force

**18 a** moon  **b** Solar System  **c** meteorite  **d** comet  **e** galaxy  **f** supernova

**19 a** cloud of dust and gas  **b** gravity  **c** fusion  **d** Red giant  **e** White dwarf

**21 a** 20 s  **b** 30 m/s  **c** 30 s  **d** 3 m/s²

## Module 12

**1 b i** c  **ii** B

**2** A and C

**3 b** changes direction

**5 b** total internal reflection  **c** binoculars

**8** E

**9 a** quicker return of echo  **b** sunken rock  **c i** 750 m  **ii** $\frac{1}{3}$ s

**10 a** B louder  **b** C higher pitch  **c** B  **d** C  **e** 1.5 m  **f** 440 Hz

**11 a** P is quieter and lower pitched than Q

**12 a** reflection of sound  **c** 340 m/s  **d** high frequency sounds we can't hear  **e** scanning unborn baby

**13 a i** 20 kHz  **ii** Y  **b i** scanning unborn babies  **ii** less dangerous  **iii** cleaning

**14 a** infrared  **b** X-rays  **c i** gamma  **ii** radio  **iii** radio  **iv** ultra violet  **v** microwaves  **vi** infrared  **vii** ultraviolet  **viii** visible light  **d i** red  **ii** violet

**15 i a** higher pitch  **b** louder  **c** different tone

**17** light, ultraviolet, gamma rays, microwaves, radioactive materials

**18 a** infra red   **b** better absorber

**19 a** negative   **b** proton   **c** positive   **d** 4
   **e** electrons

**20 a** 7 positive, 7 neutral, 7 negative   **b** same element but differing numbers of neutrons

**21 a** nucleus   **b** Geiger–Müller tube   **c** card   **d** lead

**22 a** α and β radiation   **b** lead stops all types of radiation

**23 a** rocks, e.g. granite, nuclear power stations

**24 a** electrons   **b** Geiger–Müller tube   **c** smaller
   **d** α unable to pass through paper, γ count unaffected by paper thickness

**25 a** Increase count rate, high concentration of radioactive material   **b** γ, high penetration, power needed

**26 a** nucleus   **b** time for half the sample to decay
   **c i** 400 counts per sec   **ii** 100 counts per sec

**27 i** 80 counts per sec   **ii** 40 counts per sec
   **iii** 10 counts per sec

## Exam-style Questions

**1**   **c** 80 km/h

**2**   **a** air resistance   **b** balanced forces
   **c** opens parachute   **d** deceleration
   **e** lower terminal velocity

**3**   **a** electric fire   **b** battery   **c** solar cell
   **d** microphone   **e** speaker   **f** candle

**4**   **a** can't be replaced, can be replaced   **b** oil, gas
   **c** tidal   **d** non polluting expensive initial costs

**5**   **a** 0.4 A

**6**   **a** 24 W   **b** 240 J   **c** electrical to heat and light

**7**   **a** 3 A   **b** 3 A   **c** 5 A   **d** 13 A   **e** melts

**8**   **a** neutral   **b** live   **c** yellow/green   **d** safety
   **e** fuse

**9**   **a i** £1.26   **ii** 4.2 p   **iii** 7 p
   **b** a network of pylons and cables carrying electrical energy from power stations to homes

**10 a** ammeter   **b** 2 A   **c** 4 A   **d** 6 A

**11 a** variable resistor   **b** switch   **c** ammeter
   **d** voltmeter   **e** all except 6/0.8   **g** 8 ohms

**12 a** electrical energy to heat and light energy
   **b** 36 J/s   **c** 3 A   **d** 4 Ω

**13 a** 12 km   **b** 40 minutes   **c** 24 h   **d** slower, less steep graph

**14 a** 5   **b** 2 Hz   **c** 10 cm/s

**15 a** gravitational potential energy   **b** 15 000 J
   **c** friction   **d** 750 W

**16 a** 12 V   **b** 4 Ω   **c** 2 A   **d** 8 V   **e** 4 V

**17 a** pointer 10 divisions to left   **b** no pointer movement   **c** pointer more than 10 divisions to left
   **d** magnetic field cutting through coils

**18 a** heat flows from hot to cold   **b** conduction
   **c** convection   **d** cavity wall insulation, e.g. fibreglass

**19 a** burning fuel   **c** cannot be replaced   **d** wood
   **e** increases carbon dioxide in atmosphere

**20 a** 40%   **b** heat warms water produces steam drives turbines and generators   **c** National grid

**21 a** total internal reflection   **b** endoscope

**22 a** midday   **b** middle of night   **c** dawn   **d** sunset
   **e** 1 day

**23 a** galaxy   **b** planet, comet   **c** moon, satellite
   **d** constellation   **e** Sun

**24 a** A – β, B – α, C – γ   **b** α and β   **c** α
   **d** Geiger–Müller tube

**25 a** elastic, spring, battery   **b** kinetic energy
   **c** can be replaced

**26 a** electrical, heat, kinetic   **b** 1 unit   **c** 9p

**27 a** C   **b** microwaves, infra red   **c** radio waves,
   **d** visible light   **e** skin cancer   **f** avoid exposure, e.g. wear hats, sun creams   **g** radioactive materials

**28 a** friction between runners and ice   **b** wear surface, heating

**29 b** total internal reflection   **c** 90°, 180°
   **d** prismatic periscope

## Multiple choice questions

**1**   **a** C   **b** D   **c** D   **d** C

**2**   **a** D   **b** C

**3**   **a** B   **b** B   **c** B

**4**   **a** C   **b** A   **c** B   **d** C

**5**   D

**6**   D

**7**   C

**8**   C

**9**   A

**10** C

**11** A

# Index

# Index